What My MBA
Did Not Teach Me About
MONEY

The Human and Financial Perspective
of Money, Finance, Markets, People, and Life.

SANDEEP SAHNI & SANJIT SINGH PAUL
FOREWORD BY NEERAJ CHOKSI, JT MD, NJ GROUP

INDIA • SINGAPORE • MALAYSIA

Notion Press Media Pvt Ltd

No. 50, Chettiyar Agaram Main Road,
Vanagaram, Chennai, Tamil Nadu – 600 095

First Published by Notion Press 2021
Copyright © Sandeep Sahni & Sanjit Singh Paul 2021
All Rights Reserved.

ISBN 978-1-63781-650-9

This book has been published with all efforts taken to make the material error-free after the consent of the authors. However, the authors and the publisher do not assume and hereby disclaim any liability to any party for any loss, damage, or disruption caused by errors or omissions, whether such errors or omissions result from negligence, accident, or any other cause.

While every effort has been made to avoid any mistake or omission, this publication is being sold on the condition and understanding that neither the authors nor the publishers or printers would be liable in any manner to any person by reason of any mistake or omission in this publication or for any action taken or omitted to be taken or advice rendered or accepted on the basis of this work. For any defect in printing or binding the publishers will be liable only to replace the defective copy by another copy of this work then available.

When I was young I thought that money was the most important thing in life; now that I am old I know it is.

— Oscar Wilde

Disclaimer

The contents of this book are the opinions of the authors. No part of this book should be considered as investment advice given by the authors.

Contents

Foreword	9
Preface	13
Acknowledgements	17
A Quick Note About The Authors	19
Introduction	21

Part 1: What My MBA Did Not Teach Me About Money — 27

Chapter 1	The Two Perspectives	29
Chapter 2	The Personal Finance Cycle	40
Chapter 3	The Open Secrets	47
Chapter 4	About Wealth	54
Chapter 5	Money in Relationships	60

Part 2: What My MBA Did Not Teach Me About Finance — 67

Chapter 6	The Basic Numbers	69
Chapter 7	The Crossed-Box	78

Chapter 8	The Hand of Risk	83
Chapter 9	Room for Error	90
Chapter 10	The Tide of Time	100

Part 3: What My MBA Did Not Teach Me About Markets — 109

Chapter 11	Market Cycles	111
Chapter 12	Pigeon Investing	121
Chapter 13	500 Points Movement	126
Chapter 14	Luck, Skill, and Randomness	131
Chapter 15	Everything has a Purpose	138

Part 4: What My MBA Did Not Teach Me About Me — 147

Chapter 16	We are Designed to React	149
Chapter 17	We are Designed to Ignore	156
Chapter 18	How We Make Tough Decisions	163
Chapter 19	Hopes and Dreams	171
Chapter 20	In For The Long Term	179
Chapter 21	The DIY Gap	187
Chapter 22	The Limited Menu	198

Part 5: Finer Things My MBA Did Not Teach Me — 205

Chapter 23	Don't Use a Hammer Where a Screwdriver is Required	207
Chapter 24	Read the Fine Print	213
Chapter 25	Preparing for Entrepreneurship	221

Chapter 26	The Myth of Retirement	228
Chapter 27	How to Handle Extremes	237
Chapter 28	Keeping Wealth	246
Chapter 29	Invest In and With An Advisor	257
Chapter 30	Good Advice Never Changes	264

Foreword

Mark Twain once famously said, "It ain't what you don't know that gets you into trouble, but it's what you know for sure, that just ain't so".

The quote used in the book sums up the essence of this wonderful book. What gets us into trouble are the beliefs and perspectives that we pick up over our life's journey and its experiences. The authors, Sandeep and Sanjit, have not only the technical expertise because they are from the financial services industry themselves, but also a deep understanding of the nuances of the money and investment game to explain these experiences.

Through the protagonist of the book, Sameer, they have presented interesting real-life situations regarding money decisions faced by all of us and to convey what should be the approach to these decisions. By cutting out the jargon, they have simplified some very important concepts in an easy-to-read manner.

This book is about comparing the feelings around money with the thinking around money. The "human" and "financial" perspectives are terms you will find on the cover of this book as well as all inside the book. This is a new yet very useful concept the authors have introduced. Thinking and feeling aspects are present within all of us, but the difference between them is cloudy. Separating the two is challenging and the mixing of these aspects often leads to poor money decisions. Acknowledging these concepts is perhaps the first step towards investment success.

"What my MBA Didn't teach me about Money" is a great resource to help its readers avoid some key mistakes in their investment journey. It will help investors to understand risks, take risks and also manage these risks. At the same time, it makes the readers aware that they have biases when it comes to money. It prepares a mindset to acknowledge volatility and uncertainties which happen to all of us in life and in investing. For all these shortcomings that lie within all of us, the authors have provided simple and practically applicable solutions.

Interesting quotes like, "Money is not the most important thing in life" but, "Make sure you have enough of it before you make that statement." are the hidden gems in the text which makes for very interesting reading.

Some of the common questions they have tried to answer through this Book are about:

- The role of money in the lives of people.
- What does it really mean to be wealthy for people?
- The positive and negative money experiences that come to our mind immediately.
- What to do if you come across a sudden windfall?
- Why so many of our resolutions around finances go haywire despite the best financial planning?
- Why the rich keep getting richer despite doing the same things as you are? Do the Rich behave differently, do they make the same mistakes, what drives their financial behavior?

As a learner of behavioral finance and our experience at NJ India in the "Money" business over the last 30 years has taught us the importance of increasing the knowledge of our investors and the upskilling of our partners. This goes a long way in fulfilling our fiduciary responsibility while handling investor finances. Learning is a life-long endeavour, as *Thomas Henry Huxley* said,

"Perhaps the most valuable result of all education is the ability to make yourself do the thing you have to do, when it ought to be done, whether you like it or not. It is the first lesson that ought to be learned and however early a man's training begins, it is probably the last lesson that he learns thoroughly."

To that end, I strongly recommend this book. It is a must-read not only for the investors who want to succeed financially but this book is also recommended for financial services practitioners who are looking to grow wealth for their clients.

– Neeraj Choksi,
Jt MD, NJ Group.

Preface

This book is not an attempt to criticize any MBA program or to give feedback on what should be and should not be included in any successful program. The learning and experience gained during our MBA (at Indian Institute of Management, Lucknow and Indian School of Business, Hyderabad) programs were a life changing experience for us. They gave us the confidence to face the world.

This book is a reflection on what we learnt and, more importantly, what we missed out on. In hindsight, we realized that we should have focused more on certain things, which have been discussed in this book, rather than on the routine which consumed most of our attention.

As fresh MBA graduates, we were all pepped up to change the world and face any challenge in front of us. However, harsh as it may sound, the ability to fulfil these ambitions hung primarily on the availability of money. We did not realise at that time, that the one most important thing required to change the world is financial independence.

Money is something we took for granted, we thought it was our birthright, a contract we could always exercise and that it was available in abundance. All we had to do was reach out and claim it. Yet, in the end, we miscalculated and ended up having money worries rather than the comfort of a corpus to pursue our passions. We were able to sort out some of these worries and the rest we had to live with. Therefore, we thought we should share some of these experiences and mistakes made by us. We hope to save you, the reader, from these mistakes in the area of personal finance.

Apart from our own errors regarding finances, we have encountered several investors who have made splendid mistakes as well. When we met, we often shared our experiences of dealing with investors, their biases, and their beliefs (including our own). We realized that the mistakes made by us and them, all had a common thread. Simple choices lay behind gross errors. Our attempt in writing this book is to help you avoid, or, at the very least, be aware of these missteps in your journey with money and investments. We also intend to prepare you a bit to face the glorious uncertainties that life might throw at you.

There is no doubt that our MBAs were invaluable. Over the years, we applied the fundamentals, which we learnt in our MBAs, almost 20 years apart, in our daily financial lives and especially for our personal finances. We found that while some concepts worked rather well, others were very difficult to apply, and some were even out of context.

Mark Twain once famously said,

"It ain't what you don't know that gets you in trouble, but it's what you know for sure, that just ain't so."

After working for many years in the financial industry, we observed that many actual industry practices were not taught to us in MBA. In fact, these practices seemed like common sense (once we understood them). However, common sense is not so common. We also observed that most people, MBAs or not, were completely unaware of these practices. Now, it so happens that personal finance is not taught as a subject. Most people do not really know what practices to follow when managing their own finances.

We felt the need to share some good practices and concepts. These practices and concepts are tried and applied and have endured the test of many years. Some of these practices may seem to be naive. They fall short of the sophistication that academicians would suggest. However, we opine that if it works, and it has been working, there must be something to it that academicians have not discovered yet and, therefore, have not included in our MBA curricula.

We strongly believe that we, in India, are at the right place at the right time. There is a tremendous amount of wealth that is going to be created in the next ten, twenty, thirty years, and it is up to you to reap the benefits and harvest the chronological lottery we are going to experience in the coming years. Having a good blueprint about money will help.

We strongly believe that everything is possible, however, *"the only impossible journey is the one you never begin."* We hope you will read this book and begin your investment journey with confidence and conviction. Your success will give us the most satisfaction and even if just one investor is able to achieve his financial goal after reading this book, we shall feel that our effort has not gone to waste.

Acknowledgements

A big thank you to all the people who read our versions of this book and gave us valuable feedback on how to make it better. We are grateful to all the people who have put efforts in our lives for us to experience what we have, and consequently, be able to write this book. Thank you, God!

A Quick Note About The Authors

◆

This book has two authors. Both of them are a few generations apart. Sandeep is an alumnus of Indian Institute of Management, Lucknow (IIML) from the class of 1988, and Sanjit is an alumnus of Indian School of Business, Hyderabad (ISB) from the class of 2011. Sandeep and Sanjit went to the same school - St. John's High School in Chandigarh, and are active members of its alumni association, SJOBA. That is how they came to know each other.

Sandeep studied commerce at Shri Ram College of Commerce (SRCC) in Delhi and started his career as a corporate man after IIML. He is a serial entrepreneur with a passion for finance, with interests in FMCG, Food Distribution, Cold Chain, Logistics, and Hospitality Industries. He is an active speaker on topics in finance and helps direct portfolios of his 500+ client base. The stories he narrates strikes a chord close to his heart, as they are based on events and struggles from his own life. He believes in having a holistic view of personal finance and blogs regularly on the topic to help everyone become successful at it. You can connect with him at sandeepsahni@sahayakassociates.in

Sanjit is the principal officer of a SEBI registered investment advisory. His experience in discretionary and algorithmic trading, and as a systematic investor for over 15 years, guides him to design investment strategies using multiple schools of analysis. Formulas, algorithms, and analogies speak to him, and form the core of his narrative and flow into his approach towards personal finance. Before his MBA from ISB, he studied mechanical engineering at Thapar University, Patiala. He is also a second-generation entrepreneur and runs his family venture in hospitality. When he is not busy being a finance man, he loves to observe life, ruminate on its philosophies, and capture moments for posterity with his DSLR or phone camera. You can connect with him at sanjit@modulorcapital.com

Combining narratives, numbers, and strategies to approach personal finance has been a challenge. At the end of a long, heated debate on how to explain a specific topic, both of them eventually arrived at similar solutions. The strategies offered in this book are things both of them live by themselves. They hope you enjoy reading their perspectives throughout this book.

Introduction

This book is about personal finance. It acknowledges that there is a dichotomy. Personal and finance are two words which do not gel very well.

Personal is all about you and your life. What you want from it, what you do with it; and how you realize what you want, by doing what you do. The essential tool to get what we want from life is money. Personal life is the primary objective. Money is secondary to personal life.

Finance is at the other end of the spectrum. In finance, money is the primary objective. Banks, financial markets, salaries, incomes, expenses, taxes, all talk about money. The institutions and setups do not care whether you had a good day or a bad one. They are not bothered with what is happening in your life, what your goals are, or if you live in a good house. Even your work or actions are only essential means to earn money. What you want personally does not matter to the world of finance.

We are all stuck in between this tug-of-war. On the one hand, we are driven by the needs and wants of our personal lives, and, on the other hand, we are driven by financial practices that are not friendly to our personal lives. There is a constant effort to balance these two seemingly opposite forces. It is a tough job. So we have introduced the key concept of the "Two Perspectives of Finance".

The first perspective is the "Human Perspective" (or how we feel about money), and the second one is the "Financial Perspective" (or how we think about money and how it works). Feeling and thinking about money is difficult to differentiate. In order to build that concept, you will notice that these perspectives keep on coming up, time and again, in this book. If there is only one lesson you can take away from this book, it should be the concept of the "Two Perspectives of Finance".

Inside the book

Life plays many tricks. Choices we make do not always go as per the intended plan. A business idea can be a dud, a relationship can go sour, helping a friend might be a handful more than expected, medical emergencies can crop up, even budgets for long-planned goals like children's education and their marriage can overshoot. All these choices cost us money.

While you really cannot plan everything in advance, knowing about the possibility of traps on the way and how they come into being, is half the battle won. This book talks about these uncertainties. Our intention is to give you a vocabulary around personal finance in part 1 of the book titled: *What My MBA Did Not Teach Me About Money*. Some of the frameworks and strategies we introduce here will help you navigate the territory with a map. Then there are the softer aspects of money - how you share it and how your beliefs shape your financial future. These too are discussed here.

In part 2 of the book titled: *What My MBA Did Not Teach Me About Finance*, we talk about some key concepts of finance. Trust us, we have put in a genuine effort to make it simple and easy to understand in the most non-mathematical way. Some key frameworks and strategies are discussed here. We hope you benefit from using them in the long run.

The book is slightly tilted towards stock markets because we believe that most people look towards markets for wealth creation and have most queries regarding the topic. Part 3 is titled: *What My MBA Did Not Teach Me About Markets*. We will not be teaching you stock market basics here. However, we will discuss some key behaviours of the market and what to do about those behaviours.

Investment is not all about quantitative techniques and numbers. It is about behaviour. The most common biases in human behaviour are the ones related to our money and investment habits. When it comes to money and investing, we're not always as rational as we think we are. Most economic theory is based on the belief that individuals behave in a rational manner and that all existing information is embedded in the investment process. However, information is asymmetrically known and human emotions influence investors' decision-making process. The famous value investor Benjamin Graham stated that,

"The investor's chief problem – and even his worst enemy – is likely to be himself."

Just because you are good at earning money, does not imply you are automatically good at managing it or have the right to gamble with it. We need to overcome many struggles within ourselves to get good returns and make optimum use of money. Our behaviours are our own financial enemy. Strategies to mitigate these pitfalls are discussed in part 4 titled: *What My MBA Did Not Teach Me About Me.*

The world is full of financial intellectuals who are experts in their field but are bad money managers and have committed blunders in managing their own finances. The problem is not making money, but how to handle and grow it once you have it.

Studies on rich people show that they play to win, they make their money work for them, they proactively deploy their money into the most optimum asset class, and they make their money work towards a goal. They realise that making their money work for them requires an element of risk-taking, a move out of their safe zone, and comfort with a certain level of uncertainty.

The key to intelligent risk-taking is developing financial intelligence. The way to improve the odds and become more financially intelligent is by reading up on accounting, investing, and the markets, different investment options; study the history and performance of the asset classes over time, to start with, or to simply engage an advisor who can guide you in your investment journey and help you achieve your financial goals. These are some of the themes discussed in part 5 of the book titled: *Finer Things My MBA Did Not Teach Me.*

How to use this book

The book discusses a lot of ideas and concepts in brief (and at times in detail). We understand that all of the content cannot be retained in the human mind in one go (except for those few gifted people who can). So, it is our intention that you come back again to the book from time to time. If you are using a print edition, we suggest the use of a pencil to mark things you would want to come back to or explore more about. If you are using an electronic edition, highlight, make notes. Please use Google as frequently as you like for any terms you are not familiar with.

The book has 30 chapters. The intent is to let you read a few pages every day if you read at a leisurely pace. Each of the chapters is about 5-10 pages on an average and are structured in a format wherein it starts with a problem, is followed by reason, and, finally, by a strategy to overcome the problem. These problems have been observed in real-life scenarios. We have faced these ourselves and so have the people we have advised.

To help you resonate easily with the topics, we have introduced a storyline inspired by real people we have worked with, and, at times, inspired by our own lives. Our intent is to make you easily identify with these challenges.

The reasons for why these challenges happen are scientific in nature. At no point have we tried to tell you that the occurrence of a challenge is wrong. Nothing is wrong (except if academicians say so, perhaps!), it is just that a practical solution has not been found for it as yet. The solutions and strategies we have offered are practical. They are to the best of our knowledge (and have worked for us and others we have worked with). You may accept and apply or simply reject them. Please write to us, in case you disagree, and also let us know what a better solution could be. We will be happy to acknowledge and update ourselves and this book.

Which brings us to another point about this book. We have tried to minimize and, at times, eliminate the complex jargon which finance academicians and professionals use. This book is about personal finance. It needs to be personally understood. Hence, the simplicity of language, analogies, and concepts. The book is intended for everyone who is interested in gaining some bits of knowledge or improve their personal finances.

This book also talks about the softer aspects of money and personal finance. It talks about beliefs. We understand that beliefs about money can be personal and vary from individual to individual. So we have only briefly discussed what we could not do without, to explain our point, and omitted the "*gyaan*".

We hope we have done our jobs well in bringing out the "Two Perspectives of Finance" well in this book. At the same time, we also want to thank our MBAs for giving us the skills and confidence to face the world and form a view on it.

Regards,

– Sandeep & Sanjit

PART 1

What My MBA Did Not Teach Me About MONEY

Chapter 1

The Two Perspectives

As Sameer picks up doughnuts of six different colours requested by his daughter, he gets an SMS notification from a mutual fund company. The SIP is due in two days. He looks at the SMS and reads the figure. Mentally, he notes that he needs to push it up by at least 10% more by the end of the year. He knows these small little top-ups will help him achieve his goals much faster.

At home, Priya heats water in the kettle and prepares the tray with two bags of green tea. She waits for her dear husband Sameer and the doughnuts. It's going to be, at the most, half a doughnut, she promises herself. No more, just half!

Outside the kitchen, their three-year-old, Myra, is all ready, waiting for her daddy to get her the doughnuts. She has seated her favourite toys on two chairs along the dining table. Her friends Mickey the cow and Piku the dump truck will also get a doughnut each, which she will eat later on their behalf. Priya smiles to herself knowing from whom Myra gets her taste for the doughnuts.

Sameer is 35 and Priya is 31 years old. They have been married for seven years. The second baby is due in six months. Sameer's parents are retired and live independently in Karnal, Haryana, which is two and a half hours away from his residence in Gurugram. Sameer has a younger brother Sumit, who is a voice-over artist. He lives in Mumbai with his wife, Poorni. Sameer and Sumit both take care of their parents jointly.

Sameer bought a car 5 years ago and a house 2 years ago. Together, the EMIs are comfortably covered by his salary. Sameer saves well and invests regularly through SIPs. His aspirations are to be able to do a foreign trip with his family every 3 years and buy a new car every 6 years. In the next 10 years, he wants to get his children's education taken care of and in 15 odd years their marriage expenses. For these, Sameer has planned his finances well. He is well onto his goals. Priya is currently on a break and plans to get back to her job in about a year's time after maternity. Sameer and Priya are frugal spenders and respect the money they earn.

Professionally, Sameer works for a large bank. He deals with the capital markets desk and does overall risk assessment for the portfolios of the bank's clients. Here, he is required to use his MBA and CFA skills, which involve mathematical, statistical, and risk management concepts, along with his own experience. The bank is very happy with Sameer's performance. Sameer is due to be promoted as the head of the equities risk management group for the bank's India operations. Sameer understands the markets well as an asset class. He is well versed with the risks, returns, and pitfalls of the equities markets. He thinks of markets as a set of numbers and concepts that can be managed with models and some bit of certainty, with unexpected twists from time to time.

The First Decision

Work has been smooth for Sameer. However, lately, a group of the bank's large wealth management clients, who had got together and invested in leveraged equity derivatives linked products, have suffered deep losses. The amounts invested were in the range of INR 5 million to INR 20 million. Each of these portfolios has suffered about 25% loss in value due to the recent upsets in the stock market. Certain large listed entities had defaulted on debt issued by them, causing a major credit event. The credit event has caused great turmoil in the stock markets. Consequently, the market moved much more than expected and triggered margin calls for these clients. The losses per client are not small by any measure.

The bank's wealth management team had issued a warning a few months ago. The clients, however, ignored these warnings and stayed invested in these products. Now that the credit event has happened, the markets reacted and moved sharply; they are at a great loss.

Sameer's team has now been tasked with developing a strategy to recoup these losses. They see a good opportunity to enter the equity markets. Sameer and the wealth management team know that there is no time to cry over spilt milk. They know that if they ignore the emotion of the loss, they can likely make up for these losses through the recovery moves in the stock markets. The idea has been presented to the clients. Yet again, the clients group is complicating the situation by wanting to take a leveraged position. Sameer sees that such leverage is not required at all. Yet the clients wish to be made whole again in the same way they have suffered the losses.

Sameer's boss sees his viewpoint too. He has suggested that Sameer present the clients with the various alternatives and investment options on the coming Monday. He wants him to explain clearly to the clients the merits behind the plan. This is a plan carefully and logically thought over by Sameer and will help the bank's clients make a well thought over decision.

Sameer has been thinking over this plan the entire week. However, it is the end of the week. Sameer can put the problem aside and take some time off. He and Priya too have some decisions to make.

The Second Decision

As he reaches home, he is greeted by an excited Myra who runs and hugs him. They sit on the table and it is doughnut time. Priya gets the tea and the table is set. Sameer sees that Priya's brow is up. He knows what the discussion is going to be about - Starwood Preferred Guest or Taj Inner Circle?

Sameer and Priya like to travel and stay in 5-star hotels. They are charmed by the ambience of Starwood Hotels, but also adore the hospitality of Taj Hotels. The two hotel chains are very different experiences but they now need to commit to one. This is because Sameer's credit card company has offered him a special onetime offer to buy either's membership at discounted rates. On top of it, there is a 12-month EMI option with only 1 percent nominal interest rate. Along with the purchase, Sameer will get a load of points which can be translated to other benefits.

The Starwood option is at a 35% discount, while the Taj option is at a 25% discount. Each membership is being offered for the next 5 years and the number of nights is about the same. While Taj has fewer properties abroad, Starwood has many. However, the cost of foreign travel will also be more.

Sameer has considered all these factors. He feels that the Starwood option might be better. Not only will he earn more points and get benefits on his credit card, but they will also get to have more options when they travel abroad.

However, Priya loves the easy feeling at Taj Hotels. Her mind is set on Taj. They discuss the options and Sameer makes his case for about 5 minutes. Then he simply gives up looking at Priya's face and they finalize on Taj.

Later in the evening, Sameer logs onto his laptop and opens up the website for purchasing the Taj membership. He is about to click on the payment option when a thought crosses his mind. He thinks to himself that instead of paying the EMIs over the next 12 months, he could simply invest the funds in a debt mutual fund. This fund would not only easily pay for the holiday nights they wish to book over the next 5 years, but also give them the option to choose between Starwood or Taj nights whenever they want. The thought flashes to him that in case he allocates some of the money to equity mutual funds, say about 20%, the overall gains might as well cover the cost of international travel.

He looks at Priya wanting to discuss the idea, but she is asleep already with Myra hugging her. He takes a pause looking at the comforting sight and simply shakes the thought. He returns to the screen and completes the purchase, punching his IPIN and verifying with the OTP.

The Two Perspectives of Finance

Sameer has two perspectives on money that he uses separately in order to make decisions regarding money. These perspectives are so distinct that different parts of his brain are used to put them in order. In fact, if a Chinese wall truly exists, it exists inside this risk manager's brain on how to handle money in personal life and the professional management of money.

The first perspective is personal. This is how Sameer feels about money in relation to his personal and family needs, desires and aspirations. These feelings involve his parents, his wife and child, their goals, their aspirations, and the timelines of their lives. Money here is a medium to run his life. This is the perspective which dominates Sameer's brain when making a decision about spending on a hotel membership.

This perspective is very unique to Sameer. In fact, Sameer's brother Sumit feels very differently about money, even though they have grown up together. Sameer and Priya are a modern couple. They make financial decisions jointly. So Sameer's personal finances are influenced by Priya's thoughts and values about money as well.

Priya, too, in turn, is influenced by her upbringing and her childhood experiences. For example, she holds her sister's husband, who is much older to her, in very high regard. This is because Priya was only a teenager when her sister Kirti got married. She grew up seeing her brother-in-law become extremely successful in business. She saw him build himself a lavish bungalow in Gurugram and acquire a fleet of German cars. Priya's benchmarks of a lifestyle are set up by her own elder sister and brother-in-law's lifestyle. Priya's perspective is also unique and different from that of Sameer.

Our experiences of interacting with money shape how we feel about it. At the same time, the experiences of people close to us and involved in our daily lives also influence our thoughts about money. It is a blueprint very personal to us. This is the psychological relationship we have with saving money, spending money, and sharing wealth. At times, it is difficult for others close to us to understand our perspective on money. We will call this blueprint the human perspective of money.

The human perspective of money is a soft aspect. It is fuzzy with no clearly defined rules, and it differs from person to person. The human perspective shapes up as we grow. Children start to form this perspective when they observe their parents deal with money matters, or even listen to them talk about money.

Then, as teenagers, their perspective is shaped by how they are able to spend on small things to fulfil their desires. In most households, money is rarely discussed on the family table. However, there are households in which beliefs about money are taught from the very beginning. Consequently, money may be a hushed topic for some and an open topic for others.

As we grow up and start to earn, our relationship with money once again undergoes a change. Now we are able to see the direct effect of our efforts translating into our lifestyle. The blueprint varies with age and experiences. It is dynamic, yet its basic design is formed in the early years, much out of our own control and much influenced by the environment we are brought up in.

Extreme events also influence the human perspective. For instance, a family losing the prime earning member or a businessman losing a fortune are exigent circumstances. Exigent circumstances have a deep impact on the human perspective about money. If these circumstances happen to the family when the children are young, then the children's perspectives are shaped accordingly. These experiences are intensely personal as well.

The second perspective that Sameer holds (and we all do too!) is the financial perspective. This is the perspective he is going to use in presenting the reasoning and logic of the recovery plan to the bank's clients.

Sameer deals with money as a commodity in his profession. When making risk management decisions, Sameer does not think about whose money it is and what it means to that person, or how that person feels about it, or whose lives are influenced by that money. He thinks in terms of how to act in the best way to manage the money and which rules and practices to follow. These are the thoughts dominating his mind at work.

Sameer did not just acquire these skills through experiences alone. They involved a good amount of structured learning over many years. His degrees and professional courses equipped him with some universally accepted practices on which he built more with his practical experiences.

There is typically very little argument about the tenets of the financial perspective compared to the others in his field. Only some incremental practices may differ between him and his peers in other banks, but that is about it. Mostly everyone in his role in different banks follow similar, if not identical, principles to manage risk and money.

We all have a financial perspective about money, whether we deal with it directly in our line of work or not. When we take actions in our jobs or businesses, we act towards the best interest of the firm and its stakeholders. This means we only want to grow the money in our work and try never to lose it. Therefore, we follow rules and guidelines. These guidelines emanate from the financial perspective we have acquired in a structured manner. It is how we think about money.

Square Peg in a Round Hole

We all have a dual concept about money, like Sameer. At home, money pays bills, gets food on the table, pays for shelter as rents or EMIs and utility bills. It even pays for the future of our family and their daily dose of entertainment. There are unlimited sets of choices that we can spend the money on. Most of it is done by how spending that money makes us feel. It becomes an unconscious habit.

Sameer felt that getting the membership was more important than creating a travel funding corpus. This is because Priya had already made up her mind and Sameer wanted her to be happy. He is even willing to take credit card debt as leverage and is lured by the points and the subsequent benefits he may receive. When making this expenditure, he did not think about the money being transacted, he only focused on how it would make Priya and him feel. This feeling aspect of money is related to our consumption as well, whether big or small. To our human perspective money is a means to an end.

On the other side of the spectrum is the logical and deliberately thoughtful financial perspective. Sameer understands that his clients can recoup the losses by simply buying stocks without leverage. At the same time, he knows that the clients are tempted with leverage, just because the option is available. More leverage may lead to more loss, something which can be completely avoided.

His plan is deliberately thought out and carefully constructed and not based on his feelings. There is a good amount of logical analysis running into multiple spreadsheets and projections to back it up. In the end, even though it will be a tough decision, he would have used a methodology and logic behind it because it involves a lot of money.

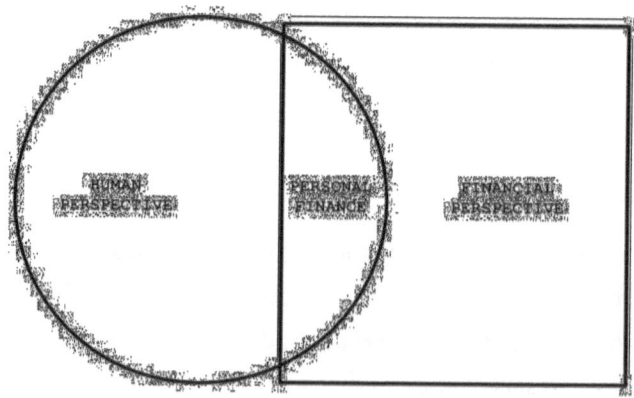

Figure 1: Personal Finance

Unfortunately, trying to use logic and reasoning to make personal money decisions is like fitting a square peg in a round hole. The wiring of our brains and the design of the world around us is rigged with pitfalls and missteps when making these decisions. Yet there is an overlap between the human perspective and the financial perspective where the world still functions, even approximately. This is the area of personal finance.

Personal Finance is Hard

Personal finance is hard because how you feel about money always gets in the way of how you should think about it. Your human perspective wants an easy solution, whereas your financial perspective wants an optimal solution. The conflict results in a financial limbo.

On top of it, personal finance is not taught anywhere. We get a lot of training to learn about language to communicate, religion to maintain moral order, personal care and hygiene to stay healthy, and even take time to learn to drive a car to transport ourselves. Unfortunately, personal finance gets ignored.

We are not educated about personal finance either. It is not taught in college and neither did we learn about it in our MBAs. We are not taught how to allocate money in our day to day living, forget alone how to save it or invest it. These are subjects which are considered readily understood as you become an adult.

If these challenges were not enough, we have our own feelings to overcome in order to make good financial decisions and stick to them. On top of it, our money beliefs are further influenced by parents, spouses, close relations, and society.

A couple of generations ago, money was considered evil and the subject was hush-hush. Later, it was talked about only as an essential. In fact, in an arranged marriage in India, prospective couples discuss topics like education, family background, religion, language, food habits, etc. Money is the last thing talked about and even then it is limited to the very basic, *"What is your salary?"* question. No one talks about spending and saving habits. So there is a stigma attached to discussing money. Yet, money is essential to living in the present and is the lifeline of our future.

Given the future uncertainty, lack of education on the topic, unavailability of organized help, and heavy involvement of feelings and beliefs around money, we tend to make personal finance decisions based on experiences. We tend to imitate and approximate some good practices and some which are exotic.

The human brain is equipped to approximate what is essential to us but not formally taught. It does this through observation and experiment. Our brains keep track of our actions and draw conclusions from their outcomes for future use. We develop a proxy set of unsaid rules around money and personal finance which govern us.

The Need for Two Perspectives

Sometimes the choices we make about our personal finances do not work out well. In hindsight, we look at these choices and realize that they were not logical. These choices were made out of the feelings we felt at that point in time. This may make us feel bad, but it is not our fault. We were not equipped with the right knowledge and tools to make those choices. We only had our limited experiences to guide us. These experiences ran short of the larger picture and needed to be upgraded. The first step in doing this is acknowledging that some upgrades are required. The second step is to use a strategy to upgrade.

The two perspectives, human and financial, are a part of this strategy. By recognizing that we can feel and think about money differently, we can overcome any gaps in our knowledge or our behaviour, and get to know what actions are to be taken. A lot can change by just looking at things differently.

This book works to give you vocabulary, concepts, frameworks, and practical strategies around the human and financial aspect of money. We simply do not intend to tell you what could be wrong or faulty. We intend to give you a practical solution to it. Many of these solutions are a part of our own learning and experiences, and many are readily available in texts. We want to highlight these solutions. Of course, you can disagree with them (and we would love to hear about it), but for practical purposes, these strategies have worked for us and people we have worked with.

Next, let's start by looking at how money flows in and out of our hands.

Chapter 2

The Personal Finance Cycle

The buzz of Delhi always excites Priya. She was brought up in West Delhi and went to Delhi University to do her B.Com. By the time she finished her undergraduate degree, computer application was an upcoming field. Priya's uncle advised her to get a Masters of Computer Applications degree. The course turned out to be a great boon and, at the end of it, she got placed in one of India's leading IT firms. IT has been her career since. She has grown well and is now in her second job since the past 4 years. The company has been supportive during her maternity break and she has a bright career ahead.

Priya's sister, Kirti, is 5 years elder to her. Kirti has been married for 15 years now. Her husband, Rahul, is a businessman. Rahul and Kirti have done very well for themselves. Rahul has made good profits in his export business and further invests those profits in commercial properties, stock markets, and venture investments. Rahul's experience in stock markets dates much further back, almost to the beginning of his career.

Together, Kirti and Rahul own an expensive bungalow in Gurugram lined with a fleet of cars which include two Mercedes-Benz and a BMW.

They haven't reached this lifestyle overnight and have done their share of hard work and struggle. It took them over 20 years to get where they are today.

Rahul says his business did him good, his savings made him rich, but it is his investments that fund their lifestyle. He says it is all about the cycle of reinvesting your gains to make bigger and bigger profits. Each cycle becomes easier and easier. He often repeats a quote by Imraan Hashmi from the movie *Jannat,* which says, "*Paisa Paise ko Kheechta hai,*" (which translates to, "Money pulls in more money").

As much as Priya admires her brother-in-law and his business acumen, she, at times, is fuzzy about the concepts her brother-in-law uses. She is unclear of what the meaning of the words income, gains, profits, savings are in context to her life. On top of it, she is clueless about the cycle Rahul refers to and how money pulls money.

Somewhere all of us know or think we know the approximate meaning of these terms. These meanings have been learnt over time and reinforced with usage. It is our human perspective at work. However, if we carefully look into our definitions, we will notice that they are mostly born out of hearsay and are not really precise. There may be a lack of clarity when we apply them to our daily lives. Hence, there is a need for a financial perspective on these ideas.

We describe these ideas as a cycle according to which money flows through our hands. Knowing what happens to our money is the key to be able to control it and make it work to our advantage. Let us take a fresh perspective, and redefine these concepts.

Personal Finance Cycle

Money already circulates in the world we live in. Each of us takes actions to interact with money. These actions have outcomes. Inflow actions like earning and investing increase the flow of money. While outflow actions like spending and harvesting (gains) decrease the flow of money. Inflow and outflow actions can be sequenced to make the personal finance cycle. The personal finance cycle can be visualized in Figure 2.

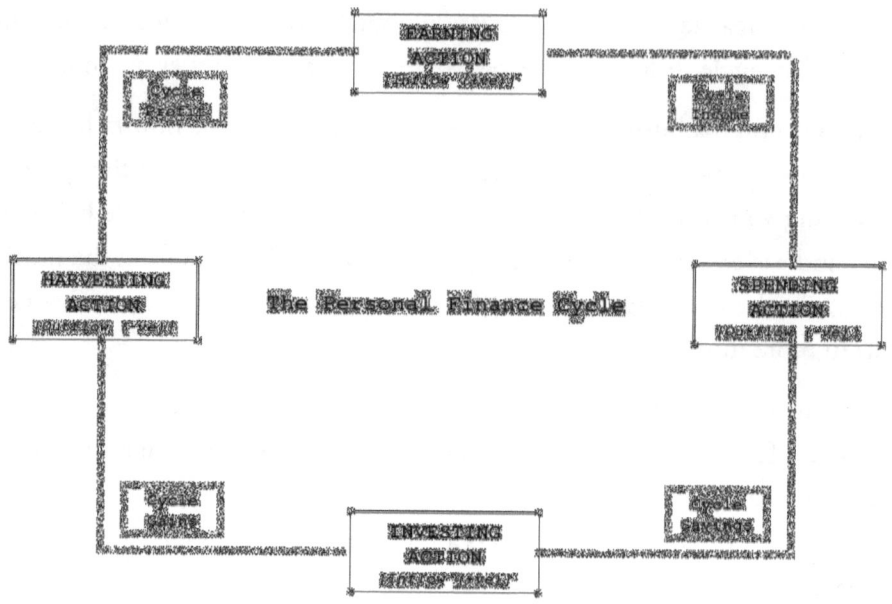

Figure 2: The Personal Finance Cycle

By understanding the actions and their outcomes, we can better control the money circulating in our personal lives.

The first action we take to interact with money is earning. Earning action includes what we do in our jobs, profession, or businesses, or any other way to make money through our own efforts. Efforts are the first booster of money in the cycle. In lieu of these efforts, we get compensated by cycle income. This is the first outcome of the cycle. If we want to boost our cycle income, we can simply bolster our efforts by working harder or upgrading our skills.

Before we are able to use our cycle income, we need to pay income tax. Income tax is an inefficiency built into the structure of the circulation of money. It can only be mitigated to some extent (legally). What is left after income tax is net income.

$$Net\ Income = Cycle\ Income - [Income\ Tax]$$

The next action in the cycle is spending. Spending action depletes some part of the net income because we use the money for our immediate needs in the form of consumption. Consumption can either be essential or nonessential. Essential consumption is required to live normally, while other excess consumption is a choice. We will discuss consumption in a bit more detail later in this chapter.

Our net income may be in excess to what we need to immediately spend. After spending for consumption, we are left with another outcome of our actions i.e., cycle savings.

Cycle Savings = Net Income − [Consumption]

Savings can be kept in the bank in the form of a savings account or bank deposits. In each case, savings can earn us interest. This interest is typically lower than the inflation rate (wait till chapter 6, where we will discuss inflation as a concept). Therefore, by keeping the money in the bank we do lose some purchasing power of that money. This is another inefficiency built into the personal finance cycle called inflation loss. Inflation loss occurs due to our behaviour of loss aversion, which could be our choice in order to keep money safe. What is left after consumption and inflation loss is net savings.

Net Savings = Cycle Savings − [Inflation Loss]

The third set of action is where things start to get interesting. If we choose not to keep all our cycle savings in the bank, then we can invest them. Investing action "may" lead to more inflow of money in our personal finance cycle.

Investing means actively taking the pain to scout for investment options (products, advisors, or managers), comparing them, making a decision, and sticking to those decisions over the life cycle of the investment. When we let an investment run its course, we are rewarded with an outcome called cycle gains. Cycle gains are the enhancement of value that happens to the money we put in an investment (instead of letting it lie in the bank).

However, if we end up making some poor investment decisions or disturb the investments before their life cycle is finished, we may end up with a capital loss. A capital loss happens because of our behaviour and can be somewhat mitigated with behavioural control. Cycle gains net off capital loss results in net gains.

$$\textit{Net Gains} = \textit{Cycle Gains} - \textit{[Capital Loss]}$$

At the end of the lifetime of an investment, we come to the final stage of actions in the personal finance cycle. These actions are called harvesting actions. Here we can choose to reap the net gains made by an investment and convert them into cycle profit. Cycle profit is the extra money we make by making good decisions, sticking to them, and also letting others work on our money. Cycle profits are the final outcome of the personal finance cycle.

However, cycle profits realized are also reduced by some percentage in the form of capital gains tax. This tax too is structural in nature and cannot be avoided if we choose to reap and use the profits. What is left is net profit.

$$\textit{Net Profit} = \textit{Cycle Profits} - \textit{[Capital Gains Tax]}$$

An alternative to harvesting actions is compounding. Compounding means we choose to plough back the cycle gains of an investment back into the same or another investment. Here, we delay realizing the profits from that investment. Compounding is the second booster in the personal finance cycle.

The Cycle's Inefficiencies

The personal finance cycle is marred by cycle inefficiencies at every stage. These inefficiencies reduce the amount of money circulating in our personal finance cycle. These are taxes, consumption, and losses. Cycle inefficiencies can be classified into three types.

1. Needs
2. Structural
3. Behavioural

The first type of drag on the cycle is needs inefficiency. These inefficiencies are essential to living a normal or good life. Consumption is a needs inefficiency. Consumption is dependent on your habits. If you live too well and beyond your means then this inefficiency becomes a problem. Living too well is a form of excess consumption.

The next is the structural inefficiencies. These inefficiencies are built into the system of making money. These are income tax which we pay on our income and capital gains tax which we pay on the profits. These inefficiencies are set by the government. So there is no escaping them.

You can only manage to reduce structural inefficiencies by a bit. Anything beyond "a bit" is illegal. For example, you can save a bit of income tax through the remedies available in the tax code. Beyond that, it is not legally possible to save tax. Similarly, you only offset capital gains with capital loss, both short term and long term respectively, (and some more techniques like tax-loss harvesting, bonus stripping, etc - till these loopholes remain open). However, you cannot hide the gains. That is illegal.

Finally, there are behavioural inefficiencies. These inefficiencies are caused by sub-optimal choices made with respect to our saving and investing decisions. While these choices are harmful to our financial health, we still make them because we are programmed to react to our insecurities, both real and perceived. We will discuss these in detail in part 4 of the book.

Inflation loss and capital loss are such inefficiencies. Inflation loss occurs when we act too risk-averse with our money and do not invest in instruments which provide higher returns than the rate of inflation. Capital loss occurs due to poor choices resulting in bad investment decisions or sometimes just pure bad luck.

Cycle Boosters

Cycle boosters are the actions that add money to our personal finance cycle. Primarily, there are only two ways in which money can be added to our cycle on a regular basis, either actively or passively.

The first way is the efforts you make through your job, profession, or business. Each one of us has to work. Even if you have inherited a large amount of wealth, you still have to work to keep it growing (else you will fall behind). The universal truth about putting in efforts to earn money is that it is limited to the number of years we work.

The second component which adds money to our personal finance cycle is compounding. Here, compounding means the reinvestment of your cycle profit from investing back into the same or new investments. If you consume the cycle profits, then you pay capital gains tax. However, if you let them be, then you let those profits work for you instead. Compounding is thus an employee who works for you. More about it in chapter 6.

To sum up, Table 1 shows the cycle inefficiencies and boosters.

Table 1: Inefficiencies and Boosters of the Personal Finance Cycle

Cycle Inefficiencies	Cycle Boosters
Needs: Consumption	Efforts
Structural: Income Tax; Capital Gains Tax	Compounding
Behavioural: Inflation Loss; Capital Loss	

The personal finance cycle is a simplified way of viewing how money circulates through your life. Of course, there can be many more actions and outcomes that happen in between. However, these are some essential ones to give you a fair picture of what happens.

Chapter 3

The Open Secrets

The rich get richer … How?

The famous aphorism by Percy Bysshe Shelly goes like this,

"… the rich get richer and the poor get poorer …"

We keep hearing this time and again from people we help in planning finances. It is almost as if there is some secret knowledge to why the personal finance cycle of the rich keeps adding more money. Whereas the common fellow seems stuck with the same amount of money and the challenges that come along with it. From simple observation, it looks like lady luck just waves her magic wand on the rich. However, there are some different phenomenon at work here.

It is also notable here to mention the Matthew effect, which states that someone who has an advantage at the beginning, will keep on reaping the benefits of that advantage. Further, these benefits will keep on adding to the advantage even more. This happens in the case of fame, opportunities given to talent, money, etc. For example, at a point of time, the Bollywood actor

Shahrukh Khan was very popular. During this era, not only did he sign up for more movies, but also got paid in increasing amounts for them. On top of it, he got to make even more money through endorsements. This is pure Matthew effect in play (though some may argue that he truly was a superior actor in comparison to most of his peers.)

In our experience, however, we have observed something different. Matthew effect works, but that is not all. Financially successful people simply focus on the right set of cycle inefficiencies (and not all inefficiencies) and make the cycle boosters work for them better in their personal finance cycle. Let us explain how.

The first difference is the focus on different types of cycle inefficiencies. We all understand that if we reduce these inefficiencies in our personal finance cycle, we will have more money. So, we work on the first two inefficiencies available to us i.e., income tax and consumption.

We work hard to save income tax (even though there are only a few remedies available to us) and to control our consumption in order to save more. This is a behaviour natural to us. Even the government incentivizes us to save more by giving us a tax break for those savings. Yet, we have not met anyone till date who got rich by saving income tax through tax saving schemes or curtailing consumption by eating less food or using a cheaper detergent to wash clothes.

The rich understand that there is only so much income tax they can save and that too can be done better by engaging the right professional. So, they leave it to these professionals. They certainly do not eat less food either.

This must mean that the rich focus on a different set of cycle inefficiencies. These can be understood by knowing the open secrets which the rich apply to get richer.

The First Open Secret: Frugality

The rich understand that the effort and discipline needed to control expenses on essential consumption is very high in comparison to the reward. They understand that the time spent on the small saving of essential consumption is way more than the money gained. So, they fix their habits and lifestyle and do not bother to change them unless really required. Instead of saving on essential consumption, they focus on curtailing excess consumption. In order to do this, the rich apply the knowledge of an open secret: frugality.

We have met super successful entrepreneurs who still buy food from the same shop, wear the same brand of clothes, go to the same barber, and live as frugally as they did 20 years ago, before they became rich. A famous example of this is Azim Premji, the founder of the multinational IT giant Wipro. Azim Premji is known to live humbly. He would still drive a Corolla till he was pushed by his senior management to buy a Mercedes, for public image. When doing so, he opted to buy a second hand Mercedes.

The same is true for Warren Buffet, who lives in the same house since the 1960s (disclaimer: it is not a small house, but we respect that he did not upgrade to a sprawling estate) and is known to have only changed his car (a Caddilac) after 10 years. Even the Silicon valley tech moguls dress in the same sartorial way by sticking to blacks, greys, and blues. They do not even change brands. Steve Jobs was known for his black polo neck. This means a rich person typically has a fairly stable consumption component devoid of any excess. This component, once stable, is seldom disturbed.

Keeping consumption stable has many benefits. It frees up the mind from making daily trivial choices. This leaves the executive part of the brain to focus on other greater things.

Of course, not everyone undertakes the right amount of consumption. Some people or households over consume and end up spending beyond their means. This needs to be fixed, but only once. Simply put, the rich are frugal spenders, not conscious consumers.

Consumables

An essential part of your spending is the day to day living expenses. These smaller items can be clubbed together and called consumables. Consumables consist of food, utility bills, rentals, day to day transport, entertainment, etc.

Consumables are necessary to live a normal life. However, consumables vary from household to household. Some households give preference to living well. They may have a good amount of spending on the food they eat or may eat out often. They may spend more on going to the movies or may have multiple content streaming subscriptions. Conversely, they may refurnish their house every 3 years or buy the latest smartphone every year. These spendings are of a purely personal nature and depend on the habits of the individuals or the family.

Consumables always give us the utility in the present. If they help us live well, they have a positive utility. However, if we live extravagantly and beyond our means, and end up hurting the budget of the household or savings and investments, then consumables give us negative utility.

Budgeting

We have observed that some households fret a lot over consumables and the budget around them. They spend a lot of time figuring out what not to consume to stay in budget. This ends up in them using a lot of time and energy in making small decisions over and over again.

There is no right way of budgeting. You can make many heads and allocate finances to these heads to set a limit. Whereas more accurate budgets will help you plan better, they are also more likely to get upset more often, especially when unexpected events occur. Also, highly detailed budgets are a pain to make, so you are likely to skip making them. Table 2 shows a practical budgeting approach if you haven't figured out one already.

Table 2: Practical Budgeting

Detailed Item List	Practical Item List
House Rent/EMI Electricity Bill/Water Bill/Cleaning Bill Society Maintenance Charges, etc.	Living Expenses
Flour/Vegetables/Poultry/Milk/Oil Takeouts/Dine outs Home delivery, etc.	Kitchen Expenses
Car EMI/Car fuel Taxi/Public transport Car maintenance, etc.	Mobility Expenses

The list above is not exhaustive. However, we recommend not having more than 5-7 items as budget heads in the practical item list. It is a well-researched fact that humans cannot process more than 5 to 7 categories of information. Anything higher than this number increases the mental load and is likely to cause you to defer the budgeting activity.

You can only save as much by regulating consumables. If the consumables are too high as a percentage of the household budget then habits of the household need to change. Most people end up axing things they like if they get too deep into budgeting. For example, if you like to have a pricey coffee every day from your favourite chain, do not axe it in order to stay within your budget. There are many more inefficiencies that can be removed such as going to a less expensive gym or working out from home. Fretting over the regulation of consumables is a wasteful and ineffective use of time. Just figure out what percentage of your income goes into consumables. We suggest that you do not spend an inordinate amount of time and energy to curtail your spending on them.

You can also simply follow the 50/30/20 budget rule popularized by Senator Elizabeth Warren in her book, *All Your Worth: The Ultimate Lifetime Money Plan.* The 50/30/20 budget rule is a simple way to budget that doesn't involve detailed budgeting categories. Instead, you spend 50% of your after-tax pay on needs, 30% on wants or luxuries, and 20% on savings or paying off debt. The percentages may vary depending on your income levels, stage of life cycle, status of your financial goals, and other such factors.

The second open secret: Risk Seeking

By moving tax and consumption aside from their focus, the rich can focus on inflation loss, capital loss, and capital gains tax. Inflation loss and capital loss are both behavioural inefficiencies. Both of these can be avoided or minimized by seeking risks and sticking to a plan.

By choosing to only optimally be risk-averse, the rich are able to earn more on their savings through investments. This means they fix up the safe component of their investment portfolio and put the rest in fairly risky stuff. (More on risk in part 2 of the book). They use a different strategy to preserve and grow their wealth called the Barbell strategy (discussed in Chapter 28).

Further, they control their urges to move out of an investment at the wrong time. This again is behavioural control. It is difficult not to react to market movements, but the rich use a slew of strategies and engage professionals to execute them. Therefore, when others are making a capital loss, the rich are hunting opportunities to compound even better, especially during Black Swan events (discussed in Chapter 27). Overall, the gains from managing these components are much greater than managing income tax or consumption. The rich simply focus on different inefficiencies than the rest.

The Third Open Secret: Compounding, not Efforts

The third difference between the rich and the rest is their focus on the type of cycle boosters. Most people focus on increasing their efforts when they want to add more money to their cycle. One of the ways in which this can be done is by getting a good education. There is no substitute for a good education to upgrade your skills at any point in time in your life. However, if you want to become rich, having a higher cycle income is not enough. You have to let compounding work for you, both in your work and in your investments.

Compounding at work means creating a setup where others' efforts can add to your cycle income. This happens when you start buying the skills which others are selling i.e., start hiring experts and professionals to carry out your work and vision.

In terms of investments, it means letting the cycle profits be channelled back to your investments for another round, over and over again. By delaying the realization of cycle profits and avoiding capital gains tax, more money can be made available to reinvest. The more number of times the money is allowed to compound, the greater is the effect of compounding. In fact, if the money is compounded by choosing the right investments in the first place, loss of money from capital loss can be avoided as well. By letting money compound, the rich ensure that they stay rich. It is their way of having even more when they already have a lot.

Simply put, the rich get richer by being frugal, seeking (the right type of) risks, and letting their money compound. That is how the rich get richer.

Chapter 4

◆

About Wealth

A Dinner Conversation

It's November. Sameer and Priya are celebrating their anniversary. This year they decided to have a get together of friends and family at their home in Gurugram. On Priya's list of invitees are her sister Kirti and her husband, Rahul, their neighbours Mrs Seema and Prof. Narinder Sharma, and some friends from work. Prof. Sharma teaches psychology and is also a scriptwriter for movies. He is often consulted by directors on the behavioural aspects of characters. Sameer too has invited his boss, Sanjoy Sen and some colleagues. The group is a motley mix of finance professionals, IT professionals, business people, and senior executives.

The guests start to arrive at around 9 p.m. Kirti and Rahul are the first to arrive. Sameer greets them at the door and Kirti quickly asks, "Sameer! What are you giving as a gift to my baby sister on this anniversary?" Sameer tells her about his dilemma. He is choosing between a holiday to Paris or a diamond broach that Priya has been eyeing for some time, or perhaps he should just invest some money in her account. Hearing this, Rahul quickly tells Sameer that investing would be the best option. Kirti gives him a frown and he instantaneously looks away and walks in.

Soon the rest of the guests start to flow in. The early winter chill, the soft music, and the open terrace invites everyone to taste the single malts collection Sameer has collected from his trips overseas. Meanwhile, Priya is busy ensuring that the supply of hors d'oeuvres is maintained and the guests are taken care of.

Sometime into the evening, the discussion moves towards the current market situation and the investment scenarios. Rohit, who is Sameer's colleague and an active trader, starts to talk about the killings he has recently made in the stock market. Overhearing his bashful boasting, someone makes a statement, "Guys, come on, money is not the most important thing in life, let us discuss something else!" Immediately there is a retort, "Make sure you have enough of it before you make this statement." Another guest chips in, "When I was young, I used to think money is the most important thing in life; now that I am old, I know it is." Seeing Prof. Sharma following the comments keenly, Sameer's boss Sanjoy intervenes and says, "Sir, what do you feel about this? You have been observing society and its stories for a very long time."

Prof Sharma takes a long sip of his drink and after some contemplation says, "Well, we all look at money differently. We have been conditioned in our growing up years to think about money in a certain way, and till today we react to it in a similar fashion." Being associated with scriptwriting, he draws an analogy, "Movies to a large extent reflect society's views. That one dialogue from the famous movie, *Deewar* in the 70s, "*Mere paas Maa Hai,*" changed an entire generation's attitude towards money." Everyone gives a laughing nod.

"Most of our movies in the black & white era had the good guys as simple village folk indebted to the rich and evil zamindars (landlords) and their munimjis (money-lenders). Think of the way a bus company was portrayed as a villain in the 1957 film, *Naya Daur*. Its arrival pushed honest buggy drivers out of business."

"Movies then reflected the neo-Gandhian and Fabian socialist Nehruvian culture that was dominant in India at that time. It is no surprise that the businessman was inevitably portrayed in a negative light. They were shown as exploiting the simple folk and were eventually taken down by the hero. Thoughts of wealth creation were definitely not for the good guys."

Prof. Sharma adjusts his stance as the guests circle around him. He continues, "Black money born of graft became the new villain in movies of the 70s and, burlesque smugglers downing VAT 69 were shown taking out notes from the safe concealed behind an idol. Suitcases of cash were associated with bribing public servants to facilitate shady deals."

"Then came a phase that somehow presented millionaires to be bad guys. Whatever the era, the villain was money. Perhaps this was because most people do not have enough of it and they have to work hard for it. See, movies just reflect the feelings of the society at a particular point in time. That is it. That is their business. But they tell us a lot about the society of that time."

"Most of you, as children, were brought up on the mantra to study hard, get a good job, get married, and take care of the family. When you were young, some institutions even taught that the love of money is the root of all evil. Further, most demands of youngsters were met with a 'we can't afford it' kind of reply." Everyone nods to this, reflecting on their childhoods.

"Then in the 70s and early 80s, the movies portrayed that all the problems in the world got resolved the moment you got a job. This reinforced a belief and became the path recommended by most parents. Doing a business was not even an option! It was only later in the movies of the 80s and 90s that wealth creation became legitimate in public opinion. I guess this was alongside the economic reformers that freed enterprises from government control in 1991. Yash Chopra, the Barjatyas, and lastly Karan Johar started portraying luxuries, wealth, and the relative comfortable attitude of the protagonist towards it. The Mercedes, palatial bungalows, and scotch slowly moved from the villain den to the hero's daily needs. I think *Dil Chahta Hai* was the first landmark movie to portray the main characters as comfortable with wealth. I think this is where the societal shift of wealth being evil to wealth being positive came in," he says moving towards the bar to refill his drink.

Picking his cue to exit the discussion Sanjoy adds in, "Wealth is definitely no longer evil. It is the need of the hour to face the uncertainties of the future. The notion that money is not everything is a remnant of things ingrained from your childhood in the 80s, and the Professor's and mine in the 60s and 70s."

Sanjoy adds, "Today, the speed of change is amazing. Life is becoming uncertain with the constant disruptions brought by technology, changing values, and support systems. Wealth is no longer evil. It is the need of the hour to face the uncertainties of the future."

Raising his hands, he says, "Look at the number of startups popping up in tier 2 and 3 cities. These are the new hubs and, here, doing a business is the new sexy. Even a generation ago, no one could have imagined that a private job, which was looked down upon, would be more coveted than any other option."

Looking at Priya, Kirti, and Sumit, Rahul adds, "You may encounter failure several times in your route to creating a business or startup. Most people never win because they're afraid of losing or failing. But don't we learn by making mistakes? I have failed many times in my business ideas, but I am on to it! Thanks to my supportive wife and in-laws."

Back with his drink, the professor continues, "For the previous generation, children were the retirement plan. The family, the government, and the society took care of most requirements even in old age and at times of need. This is no longer relevant today with the shift from joint family to nuclear family and change in mindsets. With the increase in longevity and life expectancy, I think wealth creation and retirement plan, especially, has become mandatory. So don't follow the adage that money is the cause of all evil. Don't even recite it jokingly, because what you say, your brain might start to believe."

Getting into his element again Prof. Sharma adds, "Our culture sends us two very conflicting messages about money. The first is that money is everything. Celebrity culture, the rich and famous, Dalal Street greed, the twinge of jealousy we feel when we see a house bigger than ours, or a better car. Then, there's the complete opposite message, which treats wealth and the wealthy with suspicion and envy. In some cases, it gets to the point that money is somehow considered dirty, an improper topic for conversation, and that being poor is almost a virtue. That the wealthy are thieves and their only job is to evade taxes. Only recently has the government started to acknowledge tax terrorism. All of this comes from the attitude towards wealth."

Listening intently Sanjoy's wife, Madhumita asks, "But is money really the most important element in our life?" Sanjoy replies, "I feel that dismissing money as unnecessary is a mistake. Most negative beliefs about money come from and are propagated by those who don't have it or have lost it. Perhaps there is some comfort in that justification." He shrugs and asks his wife, "Tell me, dear, what runs our lifestyle? Money or not?" Madhumita nods.

Sipping his malt the professor adds, "Money on its own is neither good nor bad. It is a means to an end. It is a means that enables you to protect yourself, to build a better life for yourself and your family, and to give back to your community. Consider money as an important tool."

Simrat, the homemaker expresses, "Money is important for me because it means being able to give my children the best – the best education, the best health care, the best start in life. Of course, when it comes to kids, money can also greatly spoil them, so I think it's up to the parents to find a way to give their kids the best, while still teaching them the value of money and not giving them an excess of it so that their view on life is forever skewed."

Looking at Priya, who is waiting to announce dinner, the professor says, "Now let me conclude by reciting a famous couplet by Rahim to reveal the real idea about money."

"Without having wealth, it is difficult to face problems. Just like a lotus would get charred by the rays of the Sun without water below it."

Everyone nods silently and starts moving towards dinner.

Chapter 5

Money in Relationships

A Panic Call

Hema calls Priya in a state of panic. Amidst tears, Hema declares to her best friend that her marriage is over. She cannot live with her husband, Bhaskar, any more. She cries that her husband has cheated on her. Questions are racing through Hema's mind, "What would happen to the children and their future?"; "How will she manage?" and many more.

Priya calms her down with comforting and braving words. She asks Hema who the other woman is? Hema replies that it is not the discovery of another woman in his life that has caused this. Stumped, Priya asks her then how Bhaskar cheated on her? Hema yowls that Bhaskar is guilty of *financial infidelity.*

Bhaskar had built up a credit card debt of hundreds of thousands of rupees. What had begun as a weekly hangout with friends for a few games of poker, had become an addiction. Hema had known and approved of the outings as Bhaskar's stress busting activity. Little did she know that Bhaskar was secretly gambling and had become addicted.

Over time, Bhaskar's bets had become large. He simply wanted to win big. When his friends refused to engage with him in his bets, he set up a completely secretive operation and moved online. A new credit card, with a new email and an official address, had been created for this addiction. Bhaskar employed Martingale betting strategies, thinking he could cover up the losses immediately by doubling his bet after every loss. The losses had racked up as dues and now had mounted to very large sums. Bhaskar had continued playing in order to recover the losses and pay off the debt from gambling gains, which had never come.

As Hema vents out, Priya tries to counter her argument to play it down. She reminds her of the time when Hema herself would indulge in *revenge buying* whenever she had a fight with Bhaskar. She had even resented that her husband would ask her the price of her branded shopping spree. Bhaskar would disapprove of anything expensive. While she preferred branded clothes and paid the premium, he would see it as vanity and a waste of money. After a few times, in order to avoid his moral discourses, Hema would hide her purchases from her husband. She would carry a tiny pair of scissors on her shopping trips, and on her way home clip-off the price tags on all her purchases.

A while later, Priya manages to calm down Hema. She suggests that such situations may happen at times. Instead of doing something rash, she should sort it out coolly and suggests that she should involve their financial advisor.

Hema takes up the suggestion. A day later, she sits with Bhaskar and their financial advisor. They agree to convert the credit card loan to a personal loan and cancel the card altogether. Bhaskar would now repay the liability in EMIs. In the end, she ends up building resentment. She fears that she may again resort to revenge spending as an act of getting back. It is no longer the same, she rues.

Financial Infidelity

Financial infidelity is a serious breach of trust in a marriage or any relationship. Secretive spending or hidden habits often spiral into starving the financial goals of the household. In our experience, financial infidelity is more common than we think. It starts as a harmless white lie when a partner or family member simply hides a sizable spend just to avoid an argument. This can escalate to more serious forms of secretive behaviour, which can jeopardize the family's long-term financial goals. There are many variations to this theme.

Hiding income from the spouse is one. There are many reasons why couples do not discuss their actual earnings with each other. Some individuals believe their earnings are not adequate, or that the wife might not respect them enough if they knew what they earned. On the other hand, there are women who think their incomes are too low compared to their husband's. They prefer to not talk about it.

Alternatively, working women can feel an exclusive entitlement to their salary and may choose not to contribute to the household by simply downplaying the topic. Lying about income happens due to a lack of trust or guilt, or fear, or embarrassment. The reasons may be many. The outcome is the same - distressed relationships.

There are many instances of people who have lost their jobs but pretended to go to "work" every day. Some lie about their income and increment, even to the spouse, to earn their acceptance or, contrastingly, to keep the expectation low. These are instances where earnings are indicators of performance, competitive status, and social acceptance. Without a marital relationship of trust and communication, the deceit gets perpetuated.

The primary reason for financial infidelity is to avoid conflict. Couples do not wish to bring into the open issues that can trigger arguments and drive a chasm in the relationship. Attitudes towards money are often moulded by upbringing and life experiences. It is the human perspective of money. Arriving at a consensus about household decisions can be tough. Money tops the list of issues where needs and values seriously differ.

Sometimes, couples just get tired of trying to get their partner to see the merits of their argument. We know of partners who financially support their parents without the knowledge of their spouse. Supporting aged and dependent parents or a sibling is a noble thing to do. It is a personal choice everyone is entitled to. Yet, people somehow feel that their spouse would not approve of such expenses, especially in a traditional household which expects women to sever their relationship with their parents after marriage. Without even asking, many women conclude that their behaviour is justified as the cause is worth the defiance. Here, simple social beliefs lead to assumptions. These assumptions further lead to actions that can cause distress in a relationship. Modern living needs modern solutions. Talk and trust go a long way.

The Three Bucket Strategy

We meet young people, who, on the verge of getting married, have queries like:

1. How should we handle our money matters?
2. How should we share the expenses?
3. Should we have joint bank accounts?
4. How do we budget for expenses and who does what?
5. How do we take care of our parents and how much can I send to them?
6. How can I support my younger sibling in their studies?

Any setup, even if agreed upon by a party, which is unfair to that party is doomed from the very beginning. This means running a household's expenses when both spouses are working is not the sole responsibility of the higher earner (traditionally, this is expected from the man). So an equitable solution needs to be used. Instead of expecting the spouse's approval for every spend, or to limit the money spent on personal shopping, it is feasible to divide the household income into three buckets. Bucket No. 1 and 3 is each spouse's individual bucket. Bucket No. 2 is the family's common bucket. The common bucket is where each individual contributes towards the family's present and future needs. Table 3 sums up the three bucket strategy:

Table 3: The Three Bucket Strategy

Bucket 1	Bucket 2	Bucket 3
Her goals.	Our Goals.	His Goals.
She contributes. His contribution is optional or a gift.	Both contribute as much as they can and decide to mutually.	He contributes. Her contribution is optional or a gift.

There is no correct proportion of contribution. Either spouse can contribute any amount to the common bucket as long as either party is not unfairly burdened, and the common goals are being optimally funded. Individual spending can vary. The spouse earning the higher income need not be obliged to contribute higher or in proportion to the income. The important thing here is to discuss the common goals, fund them, and still be entitled to your earnings.

Acknowledging the Role of Money in Relationships

Money matters are one of the prime reasons for stress in relationships and, in marriage, a prime reason why couples drift apart. Many arguments stem from the feeling that either one spouse is spending too much or is trying to control the other's spending.

There is no one right way to handle cash. The trick is to find a way that works in your marriage. This comes by acknowledging the role of money in any relationship. Here are four things we have seen work for couples who are arguing and sparring over finances.

Firstly, having a heart-to-heart chat about money goes a long way. The more effectively you can communicate the plan for your future finances, the better it is. Discuss and design effective ways to handle cash and spending together. Come clean with all things financial, instead of burying secrets.

Answer the following questions frankly and you will know where you stand in your financial fidelity with your partner.

- Do you make purchases and hide them from your partner?
- Do you pay cash so that the significant other won't know what you spend money on?
- Do you have debt or bad investments that you are hiding?
- Do you share your credit score?
- Does your spouse know what to do and whom to contact in case of a financial emergency?
- Are some of your account holdings and nominations in the name of your spouse as well?

The second step is to find common goals. Open the lines of communication. Start the discussion with open-ended questions. Make sure you share your answers to these questions, too. You'll gain an understanding of each other's values about money. Set up a regular meeting to talk about family finances. Discuss at least the following:

- Have you shared your income details and made a budget?
- Have you discussed where you want to be financially in 5 years, 10 years, and 20 years?
- Have you planned for your retirement, where do you want to settle, how much money would you require per month at present cost?
- If you have children, have you discussed what are you willing to fund for them (education, marriages, homes)?
- What do you and your partner want for yourselves, your family, and your community?
- What is the financial impact of these goals?
- For example, if you desire to travel to Europe in three years, how will you save for this goal?
- Have you agreed upon a savings and investment strategy?

Most couples spend more time discussing restaurant choices than money matters. Seeking only positives and avoiding the tough decisions are signs of a toxic relationship. Seeing where you're at on saving and spending should be a regular activity. As an exercise, go over monthly bills with your spouse, meet your financial advisor jointly, review your portfolio at the end of the year, and discuss your achievement vis-a-vis your goals.

Next, do not force a financial conversation. It can be a very unpleasant thing to do when either is not in the mood. At the same time, if both are never in the mood then it gets postponed indefinitely. Avoid that too!

We know of couples who communicate about their finances via email or Whatsapp. It works best for them to each take the time to put their thoughts in writing, and then allow their partner to review and respond at a time that's convenient. Other folks like to sit down over dinner or chat while taking a walk. There's no correct venue for these conversations, they just need to happen.

Finally, be generous. A gift or a favour goes a long way in keeping a relationship healthy. Surprises are even better.

PART 2

What My MBA Did Not Teach Me About FINANCE

Chapter 6

The Basic Numbers

A Monday Morning Dialogue With Dad

It is a Monday morning. Sameer is up by 6:30 am. He likes to get up early on Mondays so he can have some idling time before the week starts when he heads out to his office by 10:30 am. As he steps out into the living room, thinking of fixing himself a cup of coffee, he is greeted by his dad with a crisp and loud, "Good morning, Sammy!"

Sameer's parents had come to Gurugram last evening. They are going to be in the house for the next 3 days to spend time with Myra and relieve Priya so she can relax a bit. Habitually, Sameer's dad is reading the newspaper. Sameer greets him back and takes a seat next to his father on the couch. In the kitchen, Sameer's mom is preparing some tea for herself and Mr Sehrawat. Sensing that Sameer is in the living room, she calls out to him and asks him what he will have. Sameer replies stating he would love some coffee. There is always the joy and comfort of having parents in the house, he smiles to himself.

Mr Sehrawat is buried deeply into the classified section. He is looking up the apartment prices in Gurugram and is unable to comprehend the escalated per square foot rates that some of the localities carry. Compared to last year, the prices are up by a good 25%, he estimates. He sees that there are many advertisements and all of them have sharp rates. This means that there is good demand and it is a seller's market. The property prices are going to go up in the next few years. It is probably a good time to get in, he concludes. Finally, he can't resist it anymore and tells Sameer, "Sammy I think you should buy another apartment. Just for investment purposes. It will be useful for Myra's education and marriage in the next 20 years and will pay your rent as well." He continues, " In any case, your EMIs for this one is going to finish off in the next 4 years time. I think it is a good time to invest in property. It always is."

Sameer is a little slow because it's too early for him. However, he replies, "Dad, it is a financial asset world. Why would I invest in property anymore when stock markets give such handsome returns." The risk manager in him automatically adds a disclaimer, "If you invest wisely."

To this Mr Sehrawat replies, "Well, do you remember the two plots I bought in Karnal in 1991 and 1993. One of them was for Rupees 250,000 and the other was for Rupees 225,000. Those two plots eventually sold for a total of Rupees 3,200,000 in 2010. That is what paid for your American MBA degree. In fact, if we hadn't sold that, it would have fetched us Rupees 5,500,000 in 2012. However, it paid when we needed the money. That is good enough for me."

"I am telling you," he adds, "property always goes up. You will regret not entering at these prices. Plus you will get rent as well on these apartment type investments." Sameer nods. The human perspective of money wins for now. He cannot argue the fact that the two properties were bought at a good time by his father and they did fetch the money needed for his education abroad. So he replies with a simple okay and finishes his coffee. Finally, he gets up and starts his morning routine to get to work.

Compounding

The human aspect of the conversation wears off from Sameer's mind during the day. Now he is able to think clearly about what his father said from the financial perspective of money. If his father was quoting a number and basing his counter-argument on it, then there should be a comparative number he could base his argument on as well. Comparing numbers makes it easy to decide which option is better, to buy another apartment or to invest in the financial assets.

One such number is CAGR or Compounded Annual Growth Rate. This is an easy number we often use. The most common example is the bank fixed deposit rates. The fixed deposit rate is the rate at which the deposit compounds year on year (or semi-annually or quarterly). Using CAGR to compute the final amount is fairly simple. It is the compound interest formula learnt in school. You can do it manually or use the internet to find yourself a calculator. Do not worry about how the CAGR is computed. Just keep track that this is the comparable number. The formula is:

$$\textit{Future Value} = \textit{Present Value} * (1 + \textit{Rate of Return in \%} / 100) \wedge (\textit{Number of Periods})$$

Simply put, compounding refers to the reinvestment of income at the same rate of return to constantly grow the principal amount, year after year. What excites most investors in this formula, and where they wish to exert the maximum control and expect the greatest certainty, is the 'rate of return'. This is despite the fact that it is the only variable in this formula that is tentative, uncertain, and beyond the investors' control.

The two variables that are under an investor's maximum control are 'present value', or the initial investment and 'number of periods', which represents time. Out of these two variables, the investors have the most control overtime to earn the maximum return.

A practical application of the CAGR concept is in reversing the compound interest formula. If you know the starting amount of the money that you can invest and want a final amount of money, then by just plugging in the number of years, you can calculate the CAGR required. For example, if you started with Rs. 100,000 in the year 1990 and ended with Rupees 5,000,000 in 2020, which is to say your money becomes 50 times in 30 years. Then you can reduce this growth to CAGR percentage. 50 times in 30 years may look impressive, but converting it into CAGR can help compare it with some reference options. The CAGR over this period would be 13.92%.

CAGR can be compared with another CAGR of any other investment option. We can say that Rupees One Hundred Thousand becoming Rupees 5 Million is similar to the BSE SENSEX Index's growth. The BSE SENSEX, on 31 March 1990, closed at 718 and, on 31 March 2020, closed at 37,606. The CAGR in this case for the BSE SENSEX is 13.94% (even after a correction of about 40% in the markets). By simply reversing the calculation, we can convert an impressive number into a comparable one. CAGR is a useful number because it allows us to compare two investments easily. The investment with the higher CAGR is better (typically if the amount of risk is the same - which is a different story altogether).

Now, CAGR works when there is a single amount invested at the start of the period and a single amount paid out at the end of the period. However, if there are multiple points in time, where the money came out of an investment or was put into an investment, then you simply cannot compute the CAGR. You need a more advanced tool called IRR or Internal Rate of Return.

IRR is not computable with a simple formula. You will need a spreadsheet software or a financial calculator on the internet to compute the return (again do not worry about the formula, just keep the concept in mind). The IRR is perhaps the most important tool to be used for practical applications. If you have a SIP or Systematic Investment Plan, then your actual return would be based on an IRR and not the CAGR of the underlying mutual fund you are investing into. Typically, the advisor or distributor should help you compute the IRR of your SIP. The internet too is full of websites which will help you compute the IRR.

Now, if Sameer wants to understand what his father is saying regarding the real estate properties, he will have to use the IRR tool. Assuming his father made and withdrew the investment on 1 January of the respective years as shown in Table 4:

Table 4: An IRR Example

Date	Amount
1/1/1990	- Rs. 250,000/-
1/1/1993	- Rs. 225,000/-
1/1/2010	+ Rs. 3,200,000/-

The IRR for these investments would be 15.80%. This is a number he can compare with another investment, say for example the SENSEX. This means Sameer's father, Mr Sehrawat, would have got the same returns as the stock markets. Further, the supposed properties would have sold for Rupees 5,500,000 in 2012. The IRR then would have been 16.37%. Still the same in comparison to the SENSEX. Finally, considering that the property prices have not increased much in the last decade if the price in 2019 would be Rupees 7,500,000, then the IRR would be 13.76% only. This figure does not include the expenses to buy, hold, and sell the property along with other transactional and maintenance charges.

Multiple numbers seem impressive because it is difficult for us to measure the effect of time and our view gets skewed by the human perspective. Do not be impressed by a big number, especially if there is an emotional reason behind it. Simply reduce it to its compounding rate.

We also want to give a disclaimer that our MBAs did teach us about compounding, CAGR, and IRRs. Even the topic in the next section of this chapter was taught. However, using it in day to day life was up to us and we forgot about it along the way.

Discounting

The reverse of compounding is discounting. Discounts are easy to imagine because of how they are framed. Say you decide to buy a phone for Rupees 35,000. However, just before paying for it, you discover it's Rupees 2,000 cheaper at a store across the street. In this case, you are quite likely to make that trip across the street and buy the phone at the discounted price.

However, if you were buying a set of living room furniture and the price tag is Rs 150,000, you are less likely to go to a store in a different locality to buy it for Rupees 148,000. The Rupees 2,000 in this case doesn't account for much, even though the absolute amount saved is still the same. You can easily calculate that the discount in the first case was 5.71% and in the second case only 1.33%. Discounts are all about the frame of reference applied. Our brains are typically able to calculate the utility of discount without actually calculating the percentages because of the frame of reference.

Discounts become slightly complicated when they are happening over time. The most important case of continuous discounting is inflation. This means that at 5.71% inflation, after 1 year you will only be left with Rupees 33,000 to buy that 35,000 phone. We know this does not happen in reality. The numerical value of the money in the bank never goes down. Instead, it is the value of the phone that will increase to Rupees 37,000.

Inflation is a rate like CAGR. In fact, inflation is a negative CAGR. The key difference is that the effect of inflation is imaginary on the number and real on its purchasing power. This means that while you may see the numerical value of an investment grow, you will not see the decrease in the purchasing power of Rupees 150,000 over a period of time. Inflation is imaginary. Your brain is most likely not able to compute the difference, because you are focussed on the figure of 150,000.

Yet inflation exists and its effects are real. To understand this, consider the following fact. Rupees 150,000 was the starting salary of a fresh engineering graduate in a top-notch IT company in the year 2002. In 2020, it is the amount exempted from computable income for tax if invested in certain instruments. What was a whole year's salary to live a good life is now just the amount that is considered as an exemption today. Of course, the amount to live a good life today is much much higher. This is the effect of inflation. To put it simply, inflation is just the rate at which the value of your money decreases.

Real Rates

Things become a little more complicated to calculate when we get to mix up compounding rates and discount rates. Compounding pushes the value of an investment up, while inflation (discounting) pushes the purchasing value down. When both work simultaneously, we get the real rates of investment. Now life would be simple if we could just subtract the inflation rate from the compounding rate and get the net rate. But this is faulty mathematics. In reality, you will need to follow a few simple steps to compute the real rate of return on your investments. The formula works like this:

Real Rate = (100 + CAGR or IRR in Percentage Points) / (100 + Rate of Inflation in Percentage Points) – 100

This means that if your fixed deposit is earning a rate of 6.5% before tax, and the inflation is 6.70% (both figures as of January 2020), then your real rate of return is - 0.18%. This negative real rate is in line with global rates of return. There is nothing special about India in comparison to countries which give negative interest rates because their inflation rates are close to zero.

It is extremely important to know the concept of the compounding rates, inflation rates, and real rates because they are used in financial planning for goals in the distant future. It is important to know that keeping money supposedly safe in the bank is actually losing its value over time. The computation of financial goals is a mathematical exercise that is beyond the scope of this book. It is best left to a financial advisor.

Understanding the real rate of return of an investment can change your risk preferences. Even if you are risk-averse, the real rate of return will show you the cost of risk-aversion. If you keep the money in the bank and not invest it according to a plan, then with a negative real rate the purchasing power of your money will go down. We can conclude that the surest way of getting poorer with time is to do nothing with your money.

Funding a Distant Goal

Priya has saved the bulk of her salary for Myra's higher education. The cost of the higher education she hopes for Myra is Rupees 3 million today. Since Myra will be going to college in fifteen years, the cost of education will have inflated. This means that even at 7% inflation, the cost would be close to Rupees 8 million, 3 hundred thousand! This is the effect of inflation.

Priya has saved Rupees 2 million already. If she chooses to keep the amount in fixed deposit at 6%, in fifteen years the amount will become Rupees 4 million and 8 hundred thousand. What is one-third of the final goal now, will become just a bit more than half of the amount required.

Priya needs to invest in a better instrument which may entail a bit more risk. If she puts money in a debt fund and gets 7.5% returns then the amount becomes Rupees 5 million and 9 hundred thousand in 15 years. This means that if she takes this option, she still has to fund it more in the future. Alternatively, if she puts the money in a stock market large cap index fund and earns 9.5% over the next 15 years, the amount available to her will be Rupees 7 million and 8 hundred thousand, which is much closer to the Rupees 8 million 3 hundred thousand she expects to pay then.

When funding distant goals, real rates of returns show us that all behaviours, whether risk-averse or risk-seeking, come with a cost. If Priya chooses to be risk-averse and invest in fixed deposits, she will have to invest more now or work hard in the future and save more to fund her goal. Alternatively, if she takes the debt fund route or the more risky stock market route, she will reach nearer to her goal with lesser effort, but perhaps more mental discomfort.

Figure 3 shows how the real purchasing power of INR 1,000 changes over 10 years in value if it is compounded at 10% and if the inflation is 6%. Of course, over 10 years the rates of compounding would have dropped from 10% to lower. Correspondingly, the rate of inflation would also drop. Over a longer period of time, the actual purchasing power of money would grow at the real rate of return.

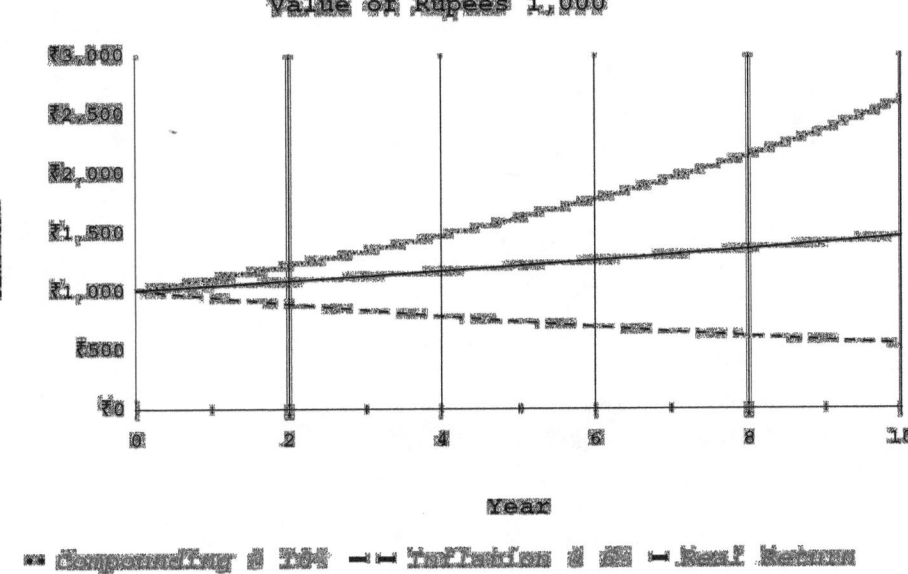

Figure 3: Compounding, Inflation and Real Rates of Return

Chapter 7

The Crossed-Box

Sameer's brother Sumit is a voice-over artist and lives in Mumbai. Sumit had worked with a startup for 6 years, but then finally moved on to pursue his dreams. Today, he is an established artist and has a large network of friends in similar lines of work. Some of his friends are advertisers working in large firms, while others are actors who appear in commercials. Sumit likes Mumbai very much. It has been almost 15 years since he first came to the city, but it was only after he became a voice-over artist that he was introduced to the love of his life, Poorni. There was no looking back after that. Poorni is from Chennai and Sumit is from New Delhi. They joke to themselves that it is the Chetan Bhagat's *2 States* story setup. Sumit and Poorni have an apartment in Andheri (W). They have been planning to grow their family for some time. However, Sumit feels that he needs to garner up some more finances for the next phase of his life.

The Dream Investment

Sumit is an open-minded person and always welcomes new things. This is a part of his character. On a Sunday afternoon, his ex-boss and mentor, Jayesh calls him and tells him that he wants to come over and share with him an investment opportunity he is excited about. Sumit too gets excited on hearing Jayesh's voice. He quickly invites him over for tea and bhajiya to his house at 5 pm.

Jayesh arrives 5 minutes to five and rings the bell. As Sumit opens the door, Jayesh is elated. He gives Sumit a big hug and tells him that his worries are going to be solved. He has come across a "once-in-a-lifetime" investment opportunity that sounds like this:

> *"You invest Rupees 100,000 today and after 1 year you get an assured return of Rupees 250,000."*

This sounds amazing! Sumit quickly calculates that if he puts the Rupees 500,000 that he had invested in a debt mutual fund at only 7% into this opportunity, he could make Rupees 1.25 million in 1 year. That would be enough to cover the expenses he foresees for the next 3-4 years for the baby. He is all set and counting the profits in his head.

In the kitchen next to the room, Poorni is preparing tea and setting up the bhajiya and chutney on the plate. She overhears the conversation and instinctively knows her husband is all excited and ready to jump the gun. Knowing Sumit too well, Poorni interrupts the conversation with the tea and bhajiya. She greets Jayesh and tells the boys to chill out a bit. It's a money matter and they should be thinking with a cool head.

Poorni is a fashion designer by profession and works with a firm in Mumbai. Even though she is not an expert in investments, she has a sense of numbers and handles the household's finances. Sumit knows his wife is smarter in such matters, so he agrees and listens to her. Poorni tells the boys to hold on to their horses regarding the investment and tells Sumit to talk to his brother Sameer. Sameer is the investments guy of the family. At the back of his mind, Sumit knows what Sameer is going to say: A big NO! He knows there is something off with this investment opportunity.

It is not just Sumit or Poorni who feel the hunch, we all know what the investment sounds like. It only takes some bit of common sense to figure it out. Yet each time something comes up and is offered "exclusively" to us, we are at the risk of getting played because of our emotions. At times, even perfectly legitimate investments can be a bad fit for us. This is because the human perspective takes over much faster than the financial perspective and clouds our thinking.

We start thinking of the outcome of the investment, rather than the journey of its life cycle. On top of it, we are all not even trained for it; finance professionals are. At times, finance professionals falter too because their human perspective takes over. What is required isn't the training to see through the faulty logic, but a strategy to quickly and easily figure out an investment. Here is one.

The Crossed-Box Strategy

Why does this investment sound too good to be true? Because it provides a single investment, with a 2.5 times reward, in a short period of time, with absolutely no risk at all! In financial terminology, the features of the investment presented translate as:

1. Low (or Zero) Risk = *Assured*
2. High Reward = *2.5x*
3. No Diversification = *Only 1 Investment*
4. Short Time = *1 year*

Now returns, which are calculated as reward per unit time (Reward ÷ Time), in this case, are stellar (a staggering 250% per annum!!!). This is akin to violating the laws of finance. Here is a real-world analogy that helps to see through this.

There is a puzzle most of us have come across in our childhood. You are given a pen and told to draw an X inside a square box with six straight lines without lifting your pen (Go ahead and try!).

You would notice that it is impossible to join all the four corners and connect the diagonals without lifting your pen or perhaps breaking the rules a bit. Simply put, it is not possible to draw the crossed box with the given rules.

Now, take the Crossed-Box from the puzzle above and put the below four words around it in any order (as shown in Figure 4):

Risk – Reward – Diversification – Time

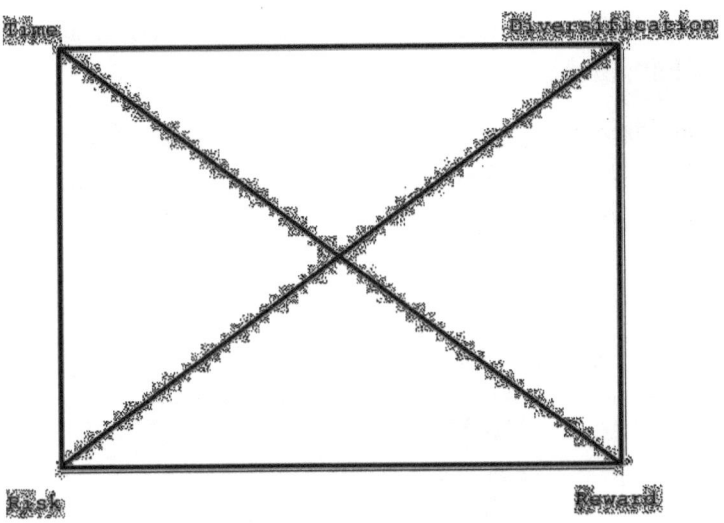

Figure 4: The Crossed-Box Strategy

We know for a fact that the Crossed-Box cannot be completed within the given rules. You simply cannot complete the figure without either crossing a line two times or lifting the pen i.e., breaking the rules. Similarly, you simply cannot have all four words in their best form together in a single investment opportunity i.e., in a legitimate investment. This means you cannot have low risk, high reward, in a short period of time, without diversification. These are the laws of finance. This is a strategy you should always remember when making your evaluation of an investment.

In your financial journey, you will make multiple investments over time. Some of those investments will give you good results to push your average returns higher and some may not work at all. Any investment which does not fit in the Crossed-Box strategy is simply not possible (or a scam). To understand why, let us look into the relationship between these words.

The Six Relationships

There are six relationships between risk, reward, time, and diversification, like the 6 lines of the crossed-box puzzle. Three of these relationships are weak and the other three are strong. The weak relationships are the research area of academicians. We will not discuss them in this book. These relationships hold sometimes, but not always. They are condition dependent.

Understanding the three strong relationships are good enough to make a great investing journey. These are discussed in the next 3 chapters. Table 5 summarizes these relationships.

Table 5: The Six Relationships in Finance

	Risk	Return	Time	Diversification
Risk	-	DIRECT & STRONG.	INVERSE but WEAK (Dependent on Diversification).	INVERSE but STRONG.
Reward	-	-	DIRECT & STRONG	INVERSE but WEAK (Dependent on Time).
Time	-	-	-	DIRECT & WEAK (Dependent on Risk & Return).
Diversification	-	-	-	-

Chapter 8

---❖---

The Hand of Risk

Risk

Perhaps the most overused and misunderstood word in finance is risk. There are numerous definitions of risk on the internet. On the day we were writing this chapter, wikipedia.org defines risk as,

> *"The potential for uncontrolled loss of something of value."*

The popular website investopedia.com defines risk as,

> *"Risk often refers to the chance an outcome or investment's actual gains will differ from an expected outcome or return. Risk includes the possibility of losing some or all of an original investment."*

The famous author Carl Richards defines risk as,

> *"Risk is what is left over when you think you have thought of everything."*

There are numerous variations of the definition of risk. Some are mathematical, while others are behavioural. Despite the importance of the term, there is no standard consensus.

This means that different groups of people follow different definitions of risk. Which implies that risk, as a word, covers more aspects than defined by most of the simple definitions. So we are content to understand that there is a general lack of vocabulary around the aspects of risk.

More words are needed which precisely define concepts which are together represented by the word risk in the context of finance. Mathematically, there is some agreement around risk. This is the use of a mathematical quantity called standard deviation. Standard deviation is a measure of the variability of the historic returns of an investment. However, standard deviation is not easy for the non-mathematical folk to make sense of.

The word reward, on the other hand, has somewhat of a consensus to its definition. Reward is the positive outcome which comes by taking a risk. It is important to note that return is a different term from reward. Return is the reward gained per unit of time elapsed.

The Risk-Reward Relationship

Risk and reward have a direct and strong relationship. This means when you are expecting more reward, then you can assume that the investment will carry more risk as well. Simply put, we can draw this as a straight line slanting upwards as shown in Figure 5. As the possibility of reward increases, so does the risk.

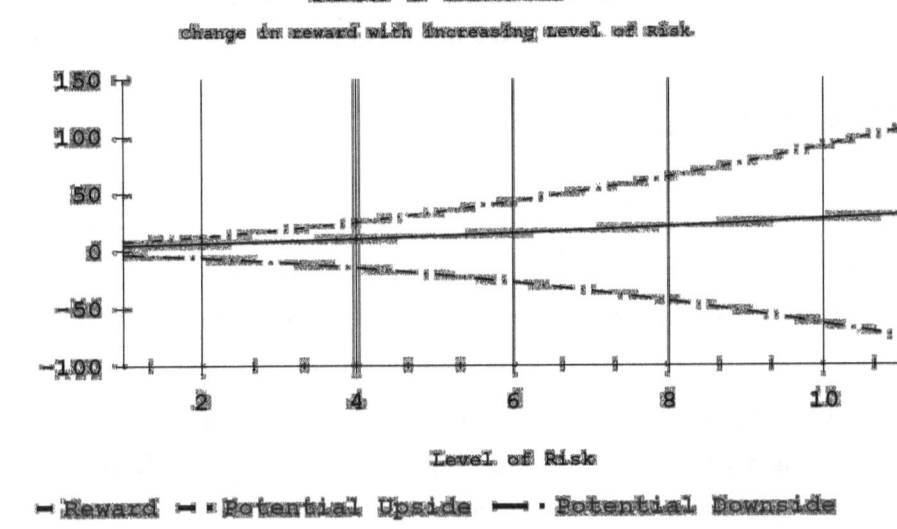

Figure 5: The Relationship between Risk and Reward

However, this straight sloping line can be elusive when understanding this relationship. The devil is in the details. While low risk "surely" carries lower reward, higher risk only carries the "potential" of higher reward. That is to say, a fixed deposit at 5% will never give 5.1% reward in a year, but the stock market may give a 16% reward when the average annual return is 12%.

The direct and strong relationship between risk and reward exists because of the laws of probability (mathematically) and the concept of risk premium (financially). However, it is our tendency to get fixated on the figure that suits us the most. For an aggressive risk-seeker, the fixation will be on the higher potential reward. For a conservative and risk-averse person, the fixation will be on the lower potential reward or loss.

The famous investor and money manager, Howard Marks in his book *The Most Important Thing*, explains the real relationship between risk and reward simply. He explains that when we say an investment is risky, it means it can have a larger variety of outcomes (both negative and positive) with different probabilities of those outcomes. The more extreme the outcome, the lesser is its probability of that outcome. This implies that you are not guaranteed to make more money if you choose a risky investment, but you will surely make less money if you choose a less risky investment.

Chasing Returns

Each of our investors, who we interact with, wants to get the highest return on their investments. More is always better. This is how we are programmed to think. It is simply an evolutionary process in play. This essentially happens because of the inherent greed in us and/or because of FOMO (Fear Of Missing Out).

In our quest for more, we seek higher and higher returns. In fact, when we see a higher return figure, we simply choose to accept it as the only reality. Everything else becomes immaterial. All other figures are irrelevant, only if the returns are higher. After a point, only returns matter and we blindly chase returns ignoring the risks that come with them. It's akin to fixing our eyes on a star and walking on rocky terrain looking upwards. We may only see the beauty of the star but miss the ditch below.

Returns are typically expressed as a compounded annual growth rate (CAGR) figure. Higher CAGR means the investment has performed better over the period the CAGR was considered. Typically, CAGR for an investment is expressed in 1-month, 3-months, 6-months, 1 year, 3 years, and 5 years. All returns are annualized. Periods less than 1 year are expressed as a projection over 1 year.

All of us, and we mean including us, get fixated on these figures to (almost) make our decisions of selecting investments. All of financial reporting too is based on these figures. Let us take the case of NIFTY50, which is India's flagship large cap index, which has been around since 1995 to understand this.

NIFTY50 has been through at least 3 major *market cycles* (a concept we will discuss in chapter 11). Over a period of around 25 years, the CAGR of NIFTY50 has been 8.91% from 1-Jan-1995 to 1-Jul-2020.

By typical reporting standards, the returns have been as follows for periods ending on 1-Jul-2020:

1-month (ann.)	3-month (ann.)	6-month (ann.)	1 year	3 year	5 year
106.61%	155.65%	-26.76%	-12.07%	3.08%	4.29%

The 1-month and 3-month returns are staggering because the market was recovering after hitting lows in March and April 2020. Longer period returns show a different picture. However, neither of these return figures give an indication as to how the future might shape up in the next 5 years. Returns may continue to stay low or reverse and perform very well.

Returns are Elusive

Returns are elusive. They are like the stars in the sky that may show us the way but do not tell us about the pitfalls on the way. Returns simply do not describe the journey taken by the investment manager to achieve them. Returns do not talk about the anxiety caused by the volatility which every investor faces.

At the same time, the above returns are historical and do not talk about other mathematical characteristics such as volatility, drawdowns, sharp ratio, betas, alpha, etc. These mathematical and statistical metrics help describe an investment more accurately. In short, the above returns hide the risks hidden behind achieving them because they cannot describe them.

Individuals do not care about these mathematical and statistical metrics because:

1. These metrics are difficult to understand and require sophistication.
2. High return figures trigger a confirmation bias. This causes us to search only for evidence which supports choosing the investment with the higher returns.
3. We assume that higher returns today or in the past will continue in the future.

In the end, we end up taking risks with a poor understanding of how the returns came into being. Some of these risks are unsavoury.

In order to understand risk better and make more informed decisions, we will present an analogy for you to remind yourself when you seek an investment offering higher returns.

The Hand of Risk

When we think of a single number, we think of a single outcome. In finance, this is a fallacy. There is never a single return outcome of an investment. Investments give a variety of returns over different periods of time. Just looking at historical returns of the immediate past can mislead investors into making poorer decisions.

A simple solution to this is thinking of more outcomes than one when considering an investment. The simple analogy to use is that of your hand. Make a fist and point it upwards. Now open your hand. The middle finger is the rate of return you are expecting. However, there are 4 other fingers which point in different directions.

The thumb points up. This is the best possible outcome of the investment. The pinkie finger points down. This is the worst possible outcome of the investment. The thumb and the pinky fingers remind us that there is a large role of luck involved in investing (more on this topic in chapter 14). They remind us that every once in a while, we can get extremely lucky and get a thumbs up and extremely unlucky and get a pinky. It is all a part of the game.

There are two more fingers. The ring finger and the index finger. These fingers tell us that we should realistically expect the outcome of our investment between the two. We should not rely on just one number i.e., the one corresponding to the middle finger.

Now, when we are putting money in a safer investment, the variation of returns represented by the five fingers decreases. Think of this as the distance of the bones of your hands in the palm of your hand. These are closer. However, when you take up riskier investments, the gap becomes much wider, as in your fingers. We call this analogy the hand of risk.

By thinking of multiple outcomes rather than a single outcome, we can make much better investing decisions. We are prepared that there will be outcomes which we may not like. This helps us in building a factor of safety when investing for a goal.

Chapter 9

Room for Error

"It is the part of a wise man to keep himself today for tomorrow, and not venture all his eggs in one basket."

Perhaps the first recorded advice for diversification was made in the Spanish book *Don Quixote* by Miguel de Cervantes in the early 1600s. In a single statement, the author gave two of the most important pieces of advice relating to personal finance. First, he tells us that the wise man is someone who keeps a part of today for tomorrow. This translates to saving or investing for the future. Secondly, he tells us to not venture all our eggs into one basket. This translates to diversify that saving or investment by not keeping it all in one place.

Even though this is the most readily available and widely known advice, it is least followed. In chapter 2, The Personal Finance Cycle, we discussed that cycle income translates to cycle savings by deducting income tax and consumption. Next, cycle saving moves to become cycle gains if we invest these savings. Finally, these cycle gains become cycle profits. It is between cycle profits and cycle savings that there exists a possibility of capital loss.

This is what Miguel de Cervantes is trying to explain. He is talking about diversification. We use diversification in our everyday life. Sumit, our voice-over artist is going to do this in his passionate hobby.

The Winning Team

The World Cup is coming. Sumit and his friends are up for a contest: building the dream team. For gamers, the excitement of the World Cup is more in the fantasy team than the match itself. Sumit is looking forward to choosing a winning team. What should his strategy be? Should he choose 7 bowlers and make do with 2 superstar batsmen, 1 all-rounder, and a keeper who can bat as well? Or should he choose more all-rounders and fewer specialists?

The World Cup is in India this time. Sumit has researched the pitches and fields, but there is a lot of variety because the contest is all over the country. Despite his knowledge, experience, and passion for the sport, can he predict the exact performance of each of the bowlers, batsmen, and fielders? Likely not.

Sumit knows that something can always go wrong, so he prepares for it. However, he cannot know the unknown factors that may come into play, like the preparation of other teams, the weather on a particular day 3 months in advance, or the health of each player on the match days, etc. Therefore, in all likelihood, Sumit is going to build a balanced team of specialist batsmen and bowlers, all-rounders, and keepers. Why? Because he cannot predict or know everything in the future and wants to cover most known aspects.

Sumit would want to keep a buffer for the known and unknown variances. He would want to keep some room for any errors in judgement he could make in guessing what the future would hold. This margin is called diversification.

The likelihood of victory increases as you prepare for the known challenges and keep a margin for the unknown challenges. Sure, this may not lead to the best performance in the short term, but in the long term, it keeps you alive and in the game.

Risk and Diversification

Risk has a strong and inverse relationship with diversification. This means certain types of (but not all) risks are reduced as your portfolio is diversified, as understood from Sumit's team analogy.

Sumit achieves diversification in his team in two parts. First, he balances batsmen and bowlers and all-rounders and always keeps a wicketkeeper. Next, even within the larger groups i.e., batsmen and bowlers, he ensures variety. His batting line-up consists of players who are long innings batsmen as well as pinch hitters. Batsmen who can play spin, and who can play pace. Next, he keeps a mix of fast-paced, medium-paced, and spin bowlers. Finally, he keeps good fielders and a wicketkeeper to stop the ball from fencing unnecessarily, save those valuable boundaries, and ensure that the ones are not converted to twos and threes by the opposition batsmen. His players will have one or more skills each, but not all the skills. So they will complement each other.

Diversification in investing is similar. It reduces the possibility of unfavourable outcomes from known and unknown risks, by keeping a balance. It is a plan for handling the unexpected in the wide variety of situations we face in life.

Keeping a balance between batsmen and bowlers is the same as asset allocation. Whereas keeping multiple sorts of batsmen or bowlers is intra-asset diversification. Finally, a wicketkeeper is similar to insurance.

Intra-Asset Diversification

In MBA, the topic of diversification is taught broadly but mostly remembered in the context of a stock portfolio. The general rule of thumb is that as the number of stocks go up in a portfolio, the company-specific risk of the stock portfolio decreases. This is practical to a certain limit, after which further diversification may not reduce the risk, but may actually only hurt returns. The famous graph looks similar to Figure 6:

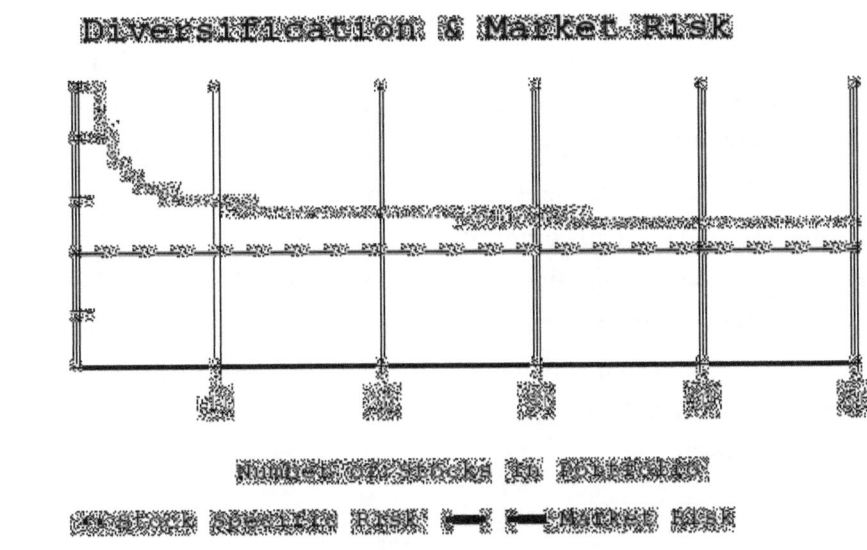

Figure 6: Stock Portfolio Diversification

Stock portfolio diversification is intra-asset diversification or diversification within the same asset class. This can be applied to fixed income or debt portfolios as well and extended to any asset class. This diversification is analogous to keeping spinners, fast pacers, and medium pacers in the bowling lineup.

Asset Allocation

Asset allocation is understood as keeping a balance between bowlers and batsman analogy. This diversification is a little less understood. However, from an investing point of view, it is more important. Asset allocation is based on the premise that stocks, bonds, cash, real estate, commodities, etc. do not move together in unison over long periods of time. This means one or more of the asset classes will move up when others are moving down. This is difficult to envisage going up and down because of the time frames involved. The cycles of asset classes are much longer than the memories and, at times, lifespans of human beings. Hence the challenge to understand its importance.

What we do not experience is difficult to grasp. Hence the human perspective approximates it. Asset allocation is often covered by simplistic models such as those based on age. For example, for a young 25-year-old, the asset allocation recommendation would be 70% equities, 20% bonds, 5% gold, and 5% cash. This seems very nice on paper, yet it is difficult to maintain because there are so many other parameters which influence the requirements of an individual or a family. These include income levels, earning members and dependants, current assets, special situations, etc. On top of this, different asset classes go up and down independently. This often disturbs asset allocation which may need re-balancing from time to time and thus incur transaction costs and taxes.

In times of crisis in a particular asset class, it becomes difficult to stick to the specific class. Equities become a bad asset class when markets crash, same with debt or gold or real estate. This causes us to react to compensate for the loss. On the contrary, when an asset class shines, then we may rush to participate in it. This is a behavioural challenge in asset allocation. We will discuss more on behaviour in part 4 of the book.

Asset allocation also changes with age or as you near the goal for which you were investing. Typically, this is to move from riskier assets to safer assets. This ensures that the goal objective is met and variation in the market does not cause you to miss the goal (because the market was down). This is a mathematical challenge in asset allocation. Models such as Glide Path investing try to solve this, but are not completely foolproof. Asset allocation is challenging and difficult. However, some asset diversification is better than none at all. It mitigates risks, even if you may not be aware of these risks.

Insurance

Finally, there are known risks that cannot be managed by any techniques of intra-asset diversification or asset allocation. Yet these risks exist. So, we have to cover these risks like a wicketkeeper covers the fence. Here insurance comes into play. An insurance covers non-diversifiable risks such as life, fire, health etc. We want to acknowledge here that the frequency at which a wicketkeeper engages to prevent the fencing of the ball is not similar to insurance. Insurance engages less frequent risks (which may not happen at all) but are known to happen and cannot be dealt with otherwise.

Everyone needs insurance, some time or the other, whether it be individuals or institutions. The All England Lawn Tennis Association, which conducts the Wimbledon tournament, has taken insurance worth $2 million every year for the past 17 years so that in case the tournament is cancelled for whatever reason, they do not suffer a major loss. In 2020, the tournament got cancelled for the first time since World War II because of the COVID-19 pandemic. The association got a payout of $142 million for the $31.7 million they had invested.

In short, insurance covers Black Swan events of life. These risks cannot be mitigated and need to be transferred to a third party for a price.

Diversification is Challenging

Diversification is challenging because of our personal constraints and the mathematics involved in computing it. Personal constraints vary from individual to individual. Limited finances is one such constraint. Ideally, you should have a finger in all asset classes. This will ensure that if one asset class performs poorly over its cycle, then another, which might be performing well, will fill in the gap. This ensures the stability of your portfolio. However, you have limited finances per year to invest. This will limit your exposure to asset classes which may require a larger ticket size to begin with.

House-Rich, Cash-Poor

Investing in large ticket items such as real estate pulls all your investment budget into one investment. This will cause the portfolio to skew itself towards one asset class and will limit your diversification. Real estate skewed portfolios are very common. Individuals may have up to 80% of their wealth in residential real estate (home equity).

Another personal constraint for diversification is the limited number of years to earn and invest. If you start building a portfolio later in life, then your options for diversification are much less than for somebody who starts early. In an ideal world, all of the diversification would happen from the very first rupee you invest. However, this does not happen. When you buy a house first and invest in other financial assets later, you are engaging this limitation. Most of your cash will go into one asset class, which does give you utility, but not any cash-flow.

On top of these constraints, it is difficult to compute mathematically how a new investment will affect your portfolio and how much you should invest in it. If this was not enough, as the events unfold and an asset class moves, its characteristics keep on changing. This would leave you to computing how well your portfolio is diversified, on a continuous basis. So these challenges need to be handled as well.

Proxies for the Challenge

Figuring the suitability of an investment is a difficult subject, given the number of constraints and computations. This is the financial perspective. When we encounter a difficult problem, instead of giving up, our brains use whatever tools available to figure out a solution. In case of diversification, the difficulty posed by the financial perspective is compensated by the human perspective of an investment.

One such tool is narratives. Most investment opportunities have a narrative. We rely on the story of an investment opportunity when it is difficult for us to understand it mathematically. Stories overrule mathematical logic. This means we are likely to be influenced by some logic marketed to us regarding the investment or other people's success and get biased in our decision-making.

Getting biased is not limited to a particular investment opportunity. Our brains get biased towards asset classes as well. Globally, this asset class is real estate. Real estate has some characteristic advantages namely: it has a large ticket size and can absorb liquidity easily, because of its illiquidity, it seldom trades below value and only goes up.

On the flip side, however, real estate is illiquid, highly cyclical, unstructured, and, if it is available in a smaller ticket size, then it is likely a poor investment. Yet, scores of individuals tend to invest in real estate because of the narratives and success stories around it. It is a prime example of our biases getting the better of our judgement.

Real estate may not be a great investment but for most people, it turns out to be the best investment they ever make because it's the only asset they leave alone and let it compound for 10, 20, 30 years. Real estate does not pay off because of how well it is located, it pays off because it is allowed to compound.

The Room for Error Strategy

Diversification provides a room for errors around our investment decisions. It can be difficult to consider and achieve. Yet is an important aspect to keep in mind when designing a new portfolio or adding investments to an existing one. However, its challenges can be overcome by keeping very few things in mind. This can be done by the room for error strategy. Answer the following two questions when you are considering an investment:

1. Ticket Size Consideration: How big is the size of the investment in comparison to your current portfolio? If it is going to be larger than 10% of the portfolio after the investment is made, then it is likely too big a chunk for you. Size of investment also correlates with its liquidity, volatility, and other characteristics. So it is a good proxy for a number of characteristics of an investment under consideration. The bigger the ticket size, the lesser its suitability for your portfolio.

2. Exposure Consideration: What is the underlying asset of the new investment? For example, for a mutual fund, this can be cash, fixed income (or bonds), equity, or even gold. You need to figure out how this new investment increases the overall exposure to the underlying asset class. If the exposure increases by more than 10%, it is a red

flag. An easy way to classify underlying asset is based on popular nomenclature like equity, debt, cash, gold, etc.

These are easier questions to ask in proxy to the tough decisions that need to be made for diversification. There are no known correct answers. The room for error strategy, with its two considerations, gives a start in the right direction.

Note: Arguments Against Diversification

Time and again, there is a talk against diversification. The argument goes like this:

> *"Most financial planners say you should diversify because it helps them to reduce the risk of your portfolio. However, reducing risk by diversifying helps the financial planner to not lose your portfolio, but that does not make you rich either!"*

A second argument goes like this:

> *"Follow what the rich do to become rich. The rich keep reinvesting in their businesses and keep a focused portfolio. Your financial planner is not rich. Do not listen to them and do not diversify. Stay with a focused portfolio instead."*

These arguments have propped up the concept that a few "high conviction ideas" are better than a broad portfolio. There is an entire market of funds which has come around this concept. Even the master investor, Warren Buffet, is misquoted on the topic. He says,

> *"Diversification is a protection against ignorance. It makes little sense if you know what you are doing."*

This is a true statement. There is no arguing with the experience and investing success of Warren Buffet. We completely believe in it too! However, you must take every word of this statement. Especially the last 7 words "*if you know what you are doing.*" But, do you? Or does the investment manager know everything? Let us understand the case of the investment manager.

There are a good number of laws and rules to ensure that publicly listed businesses report their financials and other information accurately and timely. However, most investors, including professional fund managers, cannot hope to achieve the same level of information as the management who is running the business. It is simply not possible in terms of time and quantum of information for a group of persons to know, by proxy, all information about a single business, let alone 10-15 of such businesses. High conviction ideas are therefore just overconfidence. In fact, in our experience, high conviction is a red flag for an investment (unless you are using a Barbell strategy which we will discuss in chapter 28).

There are talented professional investors who indeed know more than the average fund managers, but such investors are few and rare. An average fund manager, who thinks that he knows more than the market, is headed for a sour surprise. As an investor, you should consider yourself ignorant in comparison to Warren Buffet and other star investors. Therefore, diversification for you and for us is important.

Chapter 10

◆

The Tide of Time

Reward and Time

The final, strong relationship in the Crossed-Box Framework is between reward and time. This relationship is direct. As time passes by, the reward keeps on increasing. This means if you hold on to a good investment for longer you will get more out of it. The underlying cause of this relationship is the power of compounding. When negative and positive returns, over many years, average out, the net return is positive (for a good investment). As the net positive return flows from year to year, the power of compounding takes the reward much higher.

The key here is to remember that it all happens over time. When evaluating an investment, we often tend to fixate on the return figure, but it is also important to look at the reference time frame that return will come by. In a time period shorter than the reference time frame, returns can vary and be negative as well.

The Two Parts of the Exporter's Gift

On the 3rd of June, 2002, Rahul celebrated his 21st birthday. On this occasion, his grandfather gifted him Rupees 2 million. It was a huge sum. Rahul had just finished his B.Com degree and was ready to look for a job. However, his grandfather told him that he always wanted his son to become a business person, but Rahul's father had not been keen on business. So, he hoped his grandson would fulfil his dream. The sum of 2 million was a start towards this end, but it was Rahul's choice.

Rahul did not know whether to feel elated or burdened. On one hand, the huge sum of money meant he could have a good start and perhaps not worry about getting a job. On the other hand, he felt the weight of the dream his grandfather had entrusted him with. Rahul was confused about what to do with the money. So, he decided to talk to a few people.

The first person he talked to was his father. His father gave simple and conservative advice. Put the money in the bank in a fixed deposit and forget it for 30 years. At 8%, it would become nearly 20 million. That is 10 times the money in 30 years! Fixed deposits were the best and a tension-free investment option and had been used for generations.

However, Rahul wanted to do business as well. He wanted to put money there too. He was in two minds. So he decided to split the sum into 2 parts. The first part of Rupees 1 million, he decided to put in fixed deposits and the second he would do business with. The 1 million would become 10 million in 30 years and at least his retirement would be covered. He could try his hand at business with the rest of the amount. If it worked, he would get rich, if it did not, he would get a job and still have a nest egg. To this end, after a lot of discussions and study, he had decided to get into the export of woolen garments. It was something he felt had a good market and good potential for growth.

The decision was reached around the 21st of July, 2002. He was all set to go to the bank and start the fixed deposit. So, he called up his friend Mohit to accompany him. Mohit was Rahul's close friend from school and they had studied together at Punjab University in Chandigarh and finished their B.Com degree. Rahul and Mohit had often stood for each other through thick and thin. Mohit's father was a stock broker. Mohit was going to join his father in the business. When Mohit heard Rahul's proposition of what he was planning to do with the money, he congratulated him on deciding to go for a business. Further, he told him he would be happy to go with him to the bank, but he wanted to discuss another option with him first. So he invited him to his broking office in Karol Bagh in Delhi.

At the office, Rahul saw dozens of people on the phone shouting out quotes and making deals. They aggressively punched number strokes on their computer systems. It was an overwhelming amount of energy. At the end of the day, the busy people gave each other a high-five and congratulated each other on the amount of money they had made in the day. The market was falling and short-sellers were printing money. Rahul was awed after learning about the amounts the traders had made in a day, even when the market was falling. He told Mohit he wanted a piece of the action too. Mohit smiled and told him that they should talk to his father first.

Mohit's father, Mr Prakash, had been a broker for 15 years. When he heard Rahul's desire to trade, he smiled and told him a flat no. He told Rahul that he had chosen a good line in woolen garments and he should stick to it. Instead of trading, he should invest as now was a good time. Rahul did not know much about trading anyways. He weighed the advice and agreed.

Further, Mr Prakash told him that of the 1 million he was putting in the bank, he should only put half of it in the fixed deposit. The remainder should be put in the stock market. Rahul told Mr Prakash that he had no idea about which stocks to buy. So Mr Prakash told Rahul to buy the market through an exchange traded fund or ETF.

NIFTYBEES had been recently launched and was trading around Rupees 100 per unit. Rahul agreed and opened a DEMAT account and bought 5000 units of NIFTYBEES on 25th of July 2002 worth Rupees 5 hundred thousand. The remainder of the 5 hundred thousand was put in a fixed deposit for 5 years at 8.5% and to be renewed on expiry from time to time. Over the years, Rahul reviewed the value of his money on his birthday every year. Table 6 shows what happened to the two parts of the Rupees 1 million he invested.

Table 6: NIFTY50 ETF vs Fixed Deposit

Date	Fixed Deposit's Value (Rs.)	Multiple	NIFTY50 ETF Price	NIFTY50 ETF Value (Rs.)	Multiple
25-Jul-02	500,000.00	1.00 x	100.00	500,000.00	1.00 x
3-Jun-03	537,641.43	1.08 x	101.45	507,250.00	1.01 x
3-Jun-04	585,265.83	1.17 x	150.82	754,100.00	1.51 x
3-Jun-05	636,961.07	1.27 x	208.36	1,041,800.00	2.08 x
2-Jun-06	693,061.71	1.39 x	313.15	1,565,750.00	3.13 x
1-Jun-07	754,103.44	1.51 x	434.61	2,173,050.00	4.35 x
3-Jun-08	813,104.04	1.63 x	475.72	2,378,600.00	4.76 x
3-Jun-09	876,182.58	1.75 x	454.89	2,274,450.00	4.55 x
3-Jun-10	944,154.59	1.89 x	510.18	2,550,900.00	5.1 x
3-Jun-11	1,017,399.70	2.03 x	559.29	2,796,450.00	5.59 x
1-Jun-12	1,096,102.58	2.19 x	490.14	2,450,700.00	4.9 x
3-Jun-13	1,175,733.04	2.35 x	596.74	2,983,700.00	5.97 x
3-Jun-14	1,260,666.65	2.52 x	744.85	3,724,250.00	7.45 x
3-Jun-15	1,351,735.76	2.7 x	820.00	4,100,000.00	8.2 x
3-Jun-16	1,449,660.60	2.9 x	832.27	4,161,350.00	8.32 x
2-Jun-17	1,554,085.42	3.11 x	986.33	4,931,650.00	9.86 x
1-Jun-18	1,649,600.09	3.3 x	1109.92	5,549,600.00	11.1 x
3-Jun-19	1,751,846.10 ₹	3.5 x	1267.98	6,339,900.00	12.68 x

The fixed deposit rates dropped over time and have been calculated at 8.5%, 7.5%, 7.0%, and 6% over 5 years. The tax applicable on interest earned in FDR has also not been taken into account which shall affect the compounding as tax in FDR is on an accrual basis and tax on Equity is on redemption basis.

If we plot the graphs of the value of money on each day near Rahul's birthday, we will understand why Rahul is a rich man. Figure 7 shows the growth of money in the fixed deposit and in the NIFTY 50 ETF.

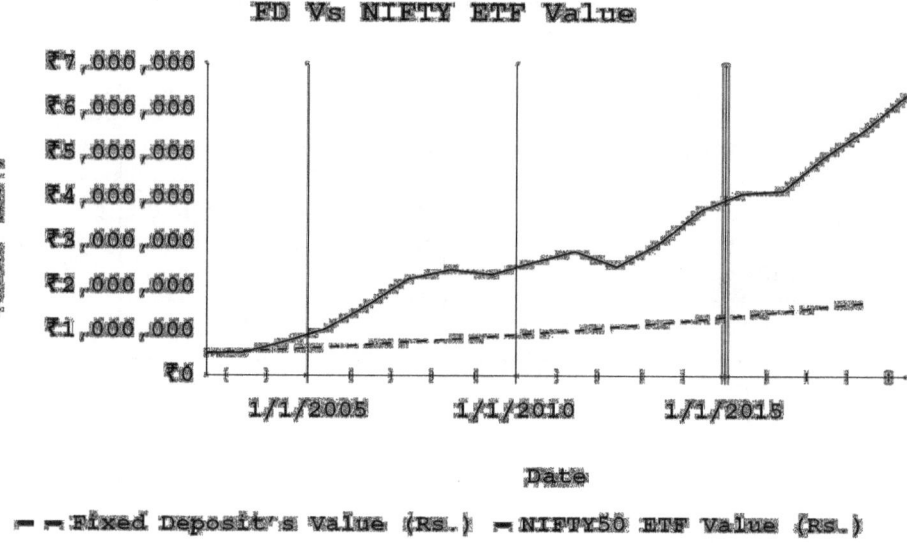

Figure 7: Nifty50 vs Fixed Deposit

It Takes Time

Rahul did not become rich overnight. Let's take a quick look at his journey and see what worked for him. The first and the most obvious thing is that he stuck to his investments. The very fact that he did not sell in times of crisis gave him good returns.

However, that is not all. Rahul was a bit lucky too. The market was pretty low in 2002. In fact, it was a bear market and remained so till 2003. If you enter investments in a bear market, they bear more fruit than otherwise. So there was a beginner's luck component which Rahul gained from. If Rahul added more amounts (which he did) in 2008-09, then he would make even more money.

By sticking around, Rahul learnt that there is a time frame after which the returns show and become consolidated. So when you are looking to invest, consider the time frame of the expected return as well. Different assets will give you different sorts of return. The graph above explains this intuitively. It shows how different types of investments vary over time and what is expected at the end of the holding period.

The final point in the above example is that the return came from an index fund, which is a diversified basket of stocks made with a fixed criterion. On the other hand, if on July 1, 2007, you had bought one of the best-performing stocks i.e., Satyam Computers at Rs. 475, you would have ended with a permanent capital loss. Bad things happen all the time in investing, some of them but not all can recover. So you have to diversify.

The Special Status of Time

The Crossed-Box framework has a special candidate: Time. Time is a factor which can influence your portfolio in a big way even though it may not be visible. With time passing by, your returns can increase many folds, the risk can go down, and the diversification can happen. To understand the role of time in finance, consider looking at it in two ways:

1. Duration Component
2. Tactical Component

Duration means the length for which an investment is kept. When you keep an investment for long enough, its power of compounding will start to show in your portfolio. The power of compounding is the most sure-shot way of getting rich, even if you do not have the skills or training to pick and evaluate investments. This is how all the investors (who put money in the markets or in their own business) got rich. Warren Buffet, Bill Gates, and even Jeff Bezos have benefitted from the length they have held on to their investments. So keep your investments for long and you will get quite a bit of the good stuff.

During this long duration of holding an investment, you are also likely to hit the chronological lottery. A chronological lottery is a sustained period of good macroeconomic and market conditions. During such periods, there are no shocks or sustained downturns and overall growth in all areas. In the stock market terminology, this is called a "Long Bull Market". It means multiple market cycles such as earnings cycle, credit cycle, consumption cycle, regulatory cycle, macroeconomic cycle, and political cycle, all coincide and perform well. These cycles, as a concept, are explained in the next chapter.

No one can figure the exact probability of when this chronological lottery will come (that is why it is a lottery). Hitting the jackpot has a lot to do with being born at the right time, and unknowingly entering the right business at the right time. Some of the greatest benefactors of such a lottery are Warren Buffet in stock markets, Bill Gates and Steve Jobs in the personal computing business, the Saudis in the crude oil business, and many more. Each of them benefitted from long (longer than 10 years) and stable conditions only because they were in the market. They got to enjoy the benefits of compounding over a long period.

The second component of time is tactical. Tactical component is also called timing or a tactical strategy in the financial markets. Tactics in markets means getting in and out of the market at approximately the right time. Tactical component is tough to manage. So, it is not for everyone. Tactical success depends a lot on the experience and the skill of the manager. This skill comes from surviving through the bad times (survivorship bias). However, those who are able to correctly time the markets make big fortunes in relatively smaller periods of time (Howard Marks has done it time and again and especially in 2008).

For an ordinary investor, timing the market is strongly "not recommended". It requires living and surviving through one or more market cycles. We will discuss more about the market cycles in the next chapter. So yes, you should not time the markets, it is the job of the professional investment manager. Also yes, the biggest fortunes in the market are made and lost by timing the markets.

We suggest that unless you are a professional investor, you should stick to the duration component of the market. It takes time to get rich through your investments. So our best advice is to start early and keep on to it!

PART 3

What My MBA Did Not Teach Me About MARKETS

Chapter 11

Market Cycles

Imagine if Sameer comes home one day and passionately tell his wife Priya that,

"Baby, markets are asynchronous, discontinuous, asymmetric, and fractal."

Ouch! Priya will probably think that her dear husband has lost his mind. She would tell Sameer that her ears would hurt if she heard these words again. We are sure your eyes hurt too while reading these words as much as it hurts us on typing them. However, the movement of the market does exhibit these characteristics. It is very difficult to describe the movement of the market in any other common terms. This is the financial perspective of market movement. Stuff which is very difficult to intuitively learn. However, markets are a common topic for any educated person and also there is media reporting that is done on markets. Consequently, the human perspective takes over and creates something proxy. Something that can sound familiar and only mildly different from our everyday language.

When you read the headlines in a finance daily or listen to a finance news channel, they cover a lot about the movement of the market. The media describes the movement in great detail. Some of the common terminologies used are trend, gap-up/gap-down, critical levels, bullish/bearish, volatile, sideways, 52-week high/low, 200 DMA, put call ratio, etc.

This is the general public's vocabulary. The human perspective of financial markets. It is limited to common words which make the visualization of market movement easy. This is because the common person does not understand technical terms. It would require them to undergo some training in mathematics and finance to be remotely able to understand the technical terms. (You can praise us for not using those terms again. We promised!)

Consequently, most of what we know about market movement is as per the common descriptions available. Yet it is important to learn about the real nature of markets to be able to invest in them and profit from them. So we start with one term – cyclical. It is a term which is easy to visualize and understand. We can confidently say that markets are cyclical. Let us understand how.

Market Cycles

Up and down – that is the motion of the stock prices, the index prices, the commodities' prices, the bond prices, the currency prices, and any traded price possible. Our brains have evolved to identify and determine patterns in everything we see or hear or experience. We see cycles in stock markets too. Markets going up and coming down is "almost" rhythmic, even though in the long term, the overall drift of the market is upwards.

A graph of the NIFTY50 index in Figure 8 shows that it goes up and down in sequence like a cycle. However, it is almost a cycle but not a perfect one. You will notice that the market:

1. Does not go up and down evenly; there is always a bias towards the upper side;
2. The up periods are slow and the down periods are fast;

3. At times the direction changes suddenly;
4. If you zoom in from one time frame to a faster time frame the shape will seem the same.

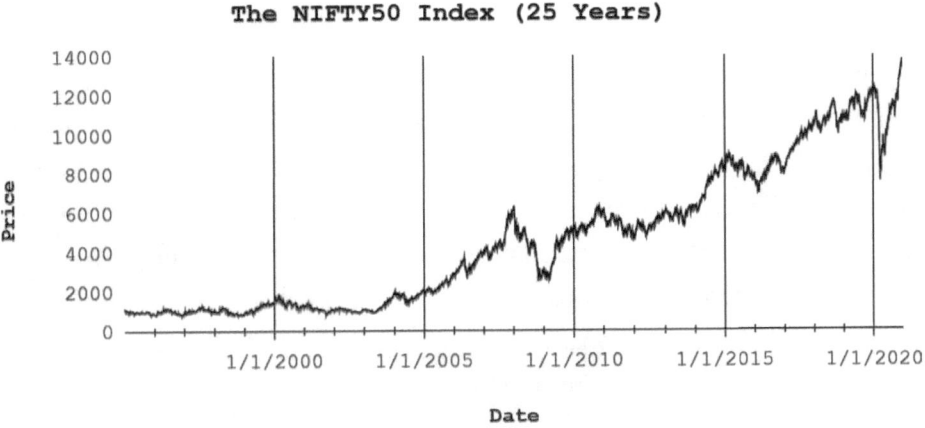

Figure 8: NIFTY50 Plot over 25 years showing a cyclical movement

Overall, the market seems to go up only in the long run. You would make money if you held on to the market for long enough – but that is another story. Then why in the shorter run does the market go down when it has to eventually go up? This is a question that has baffled many intellectuals, experts, and gurus. We too do not know exactly why. However, we do know of a few cycles which are observable when the market goes up and down. Knowing about these cycles helps explain why markets are going up or down. This knowledge is important for investing. The important thing to remember here is that these cycles are not perfect over time or magnitude.

Earnings Cycle

The first cycle pertains to the future profits of businesses. When businesses make profits, markets go up. When analysts expect businesses to make even more profits, markets go even higher. Subsequently, when businesses make less profits or losses or are expected to perform poorly, then markets go down.

This is the earnings cycle. Interestingly, almost all different types of businesses make more or less profits at nearly the same time. This is because their profits are linked to the credit markets and consumer behaviour.

Credit Cycle

When banks and other financial institutions provide easy terms of credit to businesses, they expand and grow their reach. This brings in more profits. So when credit is easy flowing, markets go up and vice versa. This is the credit cycle. At its peak, credit comes easy. Even the poorest of proposals get funded. It is almost like nobody wants to miss the lending party. You may personally notice that lending institutions may call you or email you or send you SMSs offering credit cards, personal loans, and other offers. This is an easy credit available. Then, at its bottom, nobody wants to lend, even to the soundest of proposals. Banks say no, lending rates shoot up, and everyone wants to be highly sceptical.

Consumption Cycle

At the same time, because the banks are lending, consumers may take up loans to finance their purchases or even spend their savings to consume. Most of this spending is done by consumers because of the good vibes which are created by the spending of everyone else around them. In good times, consumers find comfort in the fact that they have stable income sources which will last forever. The wealth effect also comes into play here. The inflated value of the consumer's assets makes them feel rich. Consequently, they want to spend like a rich person. The good vibes, the stable incomes, and wealth effect make the consumer believe that they can spend today and replenish it tomorrow. So their spending brings in profits and markets go up further. This is the consumption cycle.

Regulatory Cycle

Now banks and other institutions need to have more money in order to lend more. This amount is regulated by the central banks through its policy.

The central bank can raise the rates and banks will lend less or can loosen the rates so banks can lend more. This policy is dictated by the directive of the central bank. In the case of India, it is inflation and growth (consumption). If inflation is low, the policy will be loose so that growth can happen, and vice versa.

Macroeconomic Cycle

Of course, the government is involved too. The government makes plans about its spending or taxes or various other schemes which boost an industry or curtail it. The government makes these decisions based on macroeconomic data which consists of figures such as GDP, national income, etc. The macroeconomic data is purely a measurement and tells us what has happened. Based on this data, the government makes the next year's budget. If the data is good, we get more schemes and incentives, if it is bad, then we get prudence measures. This is the macroeconomic cycle.

Political Cycle

Now the government can be left, right, or centre in its views and promises. Accordingly, it makes its policies based on the political promises it made when it came to power. Since we may not have the same government in succession, and views can vary between the centre and the states, we can assume that the markets are influenced by the political cycle as well.

Sentiment Cycle

Finally, in the short run, the investors hear the news and react to it. This is because we have an urgency instinct. This instinct is described by Hans Rosling in his book *Factfulness*. We feel the urge to act when we hear something important or at least deemed important by our minds. So in the short run, any news about these cycles i.e., earnings, credit, consumption, regulatory, macroeconomic, and politics makes us react. When all of us who hear the news and react in a similar way, the markets may go up or down sharply. This is the sentiment cycle.

There are numerous other cycles that affect the markets like the real estate cycle, cycles in risk attitudes, distressed debt, etc. A detailed study of these is given in the book, *Mastering the Market Cycle* by Howard Marks. Our explanation of the cycles is simplified for you to form a fair idea of these concepts. In their entirety, the cycles are a complex system with feedback loops.

The cycles described above vary in their:

1. Frequency (How fast they go up or down),
2. Magnitude (How much they go up or down), and,
3. Underlying trend (Appearing to drift in an upward or downward direction for a long time).

When all the cycles described above combine, they form the market cycle. This cycle is jagged in shape because it is the consequence of many influences. Practically, it is impossible to precisely predict when and by how much will the market cycle swing in a direction. However, the direction and the broad timing of that direction can be estimated for a short future period. What is more important is to internalize the fact that markets are cyclical in nature. Keep in mind 2 points:

1. Markets go up and down.
2. This happens with all sorts of markets, not just the stock markets.

Profiting from Market Cycles

You can adopt two strategies to benefit from the market cycles. The first strategy is described in the previous chapter i.e., tactical strategy or timing the market. This means you can exit or lessen your position near the top of the cycle and load up your position near the bottom. It is impossible to predict the exact top and bottom. However, some approximation through mathematics and statistics can be made. This requires skill, training, and discipline. It is not everyone's cup of tea. In fact, we recommend that you do not engage in this strategy. The best thing to do is to find a money manager who can, and allocate only some of your portfolio to them.

The second strategy is time staggering your investments i.e., using a SIP. A systematic investment plan (SIP) or systematic transfer plan (STP) means that you ignore the cycle and keep adding a position to your investment corpus. Over a period of time (i.e., 1 full cycle), some of these investments will have entered at a low rate and some at a high rate. It postulates that you are likely to get the average rate if you are consistent in your investing.

However, there is one anomaly that cannot be covered. The asymmetric nature of the market cycle. The market goes up slowly and comes down fast. This means more of your capital, which is being deployed through a SIP or STP, is going to be invested at rates above the average rate rather than below it. Let us understand this with the example of Rahul's investment, which he started in 2002. What if Rahul did not invest the entire Rupees 500,000 in one go but did the same in an STP (Systematic Transfer Plan) from the fixed deposit at Rupees 10,000 per month. That means he would have been fully invested in 61 months (assuming the interest component for about Rupees 101,711 earned from fixed deposits, while the money which was not invested, was ploughed back into the markets).

On 3rd June 2019, he would have landed with approximately Rupees 4.15 million. This would be significantly lower than Rupees 6.33 million if he had invested the entire amount in 1 go (lump-sum investment). So, in this case, the systematic transfer plan would not have been an optimal solution. So when should you SIP, STP, SEP, or SWP?

Which S*P? When?

Systematic plans are basic tools to overcome the inability of the common investor or financial planner to time the markets well and enter the markets in a disciplined manner when lump-sum investment is not available. There are various studies and cases built around how well they are suited to each investor. We would not argue with the numerous studies and case studies around the SIP, STP, and SWP. However, not every type of system is applicable to every situation. Table 7 summarizes some basic principles to follow so that you do not misuse these systematic tools.

Table 7: Systematic Plans

System	When to Use.	When not to Use.
SIP - Systematic Investment Plan	When you simply do not have a lump sum investment to start with. SIP is a great tool to get investing in the markets as and when the money comes. This brings financial discipline and overcomes fear/ greed.	If you have a lump sum, do not average. You can consult an advisor or a fund manager to know when is a good time to enter. If the markets are heated, it makes sense to wait and enter at an opportune time. Staggering entry over long periods of a rising market is not really wise. Markets give entries, enter lump sum then.
	SIPs are great for investing in portfolios. These can be Index Funds or ETFs, Mutual Funds or a Stock Portfolio investing strategy.	Do not use a SIP (or SEP - Systematic Equity Plan) to enter a single stock position. SIP in a stock is a form of averaging. You might feel good when the stock is falling and you are able to build a larger position for the same amount of money. However, if the stock does not come back up, you will be left with a large amount of undesirable stuff.
STP - Systematic Transfer Plan	When you are jumping within a similar asset class or funds. For example, if you are switching from Mid Caps to Large Caps you can use an STP. This is because the market cycles of both these equity sub-classes are correlated.	When you are moving between two uncorrelated asset classes do not use an STP. Especially if you are going to change from debt to equity, do not use STP. Use the principles of lump sum investing instead.

SWP - Systematic Withdrawal Plan	When you are trying to create income from your investments in debt. Debt has a fixed coupon as income. Ideally, you should withdraw the coupon amount or less to keep the principal intact.	An SWP should never be used with a cyclical asset like equity. When the market is going up, you can withdraw and the principal amount may replenish still. However, if the market is going down you will be badly damaging your principal amount.

Dynamic Allocation

The true tool to profit from cycles is dynamic allocation. Dynamic allocation simply means that the amount of investment that goes into a particular asset varies according to the asset's specific cycle. If the asset is relatively expensive at that point in time, then you allocate less capital to it. On the other hand, if it is relatively cheap, then you allocate more capital to it. The amount of capital allocated keeps changing with time and market conditions. In order to effectuate this variation, there needs to be a consistent and reliable formula according to which capital allocation is done.

The second component in dynamic allocation is the alternate asset (not alternative asset). An alternate asset typically has a complimentary cycle to the primary asset. Ideally, it should be cheap when the primary asset is expensive and vice versa.

If 100% capital is not going into the primary asset, then the balance needs to be put in another asset. It will take some understanding of the dynamic asset allocation formula to figure out what is the alternate asset to park funds, meanwhile, when to allocate more or less and how. These are steps that should be taken under advice only.

A popular combination used for dynamic allocation is an equity-debt duo. The underlying formula is price to earnings ratio (or P/E ratio) of the index such as the Nifty50. When the P/E of the index is low, more allocation is done to equity and lesser to debt. As the cycle progresses for equity, the P/E keeps on going up. Consequently, lesser allocation is done to equity and more is done to debt.

Thus dynamic allocation based on a formula is perhaps the easiest way to capture the market cycle. However, a lot depends on the formula and its underlying metric. In case of the P/E, care should be taken that the Index P/E is dependent on the stocks that constitute the index. The stocks keep changing from time to time. This means the characteristics of the formula changes as well.

Given the technical nature of dynamic allocation, it is best managed by a good money manager or automated. You, as an investor, should focus on selecting the right manager or system.

Chapter 12

Pigeon Investing

Pigeons in the Park

On a sunny winter afternoon, Priya decided to take Myra to the park and soak up the sun. Myra would play with the children and Priya would chat with the ladies in the neighbourhood. It was 3.30 pm. Priya figured the ladies would not come at least till 4 p.m. So, she thought to herself that in the meantime she would feed the pigeons. She packed a few handfuls of grains in a paper bag and put them in the backpack which was filled with Myra's supplies.

At the park, Priya set herself up on a bench in the full sun. She let Myra go free so that she could run around and play. Priya knew that the pigeons would not eat from her hand, so she spread the grains on the ground where they could come and peck. After a short while, a few pigeons came and started to peck. Even before the first few had barely started, a lot more flew in. Soon they were all climbing on top of each other and were busily competing to feed themselves.

A while later, Myra also saw the flock of pigeons sitting on the ground pecking at grains. Attracted by the sight, the innocent child ran towards the pigeons to observe them closely and probably catch hold of one of them. The pigeons perceived this as a threat. Immediately, the nearest few started to fly away and, within moments, the entire flock followed in the same direction. By the time Myra reached the spot, the pigeons were all off. So she came back walking to her mother to sit with her. After a while, the pigeons again saw the coast was clear and landed back on the spot to peck the grains again. Priya lazily observed the pigeons' behaviour.

A few minutes later, the same flock of grain-pecking pigeons spotted a cat charging towards them. The cat was hungry and saw an opportunity to make a meal of one of the pigeons. What did the pigeons do? They flew away together in the same direction and then in a circle. When the cat was unsuccessful in catching any of the pigeons, it gave up, jumped over the fence, and went to the next park across the road. Priya soon observed that the pigeons once again settled at the same spot and were again on top of each other to peck the grains.

The pigeons were pecking away merrily. Why not, after all, it's easy food. A whole bunch huddled together. This time, an eagle flew overhead. The eagle was also hungry and wanted to make a meal of one of the pigeons. It swiftly swooped down and caught one pigeon. What did the pigeons do? The same thing. They flew away together in the same direction and then in a circle, only to land back at the same spot.

Fifteen minutes later the eagle was full. It again went on a flight. Seeing its shadow on the ground, the pigeons got startled and their flight response triggered. They flew only to circle back on to the grains once again. Priya observed the same behaviour over and over again. It was a different threat or the perception of it each time, but the reaction was the same.

Predictable Irrationality

Investors also behave like a flock of pigeons. The grains are the bull market's returns; easy and spread over the ground, ready to be pecked. A bull market is the best place to grow capital. However, whenever investors perceive any threat, they do one sure-shot thing. They sell their holdings, salvage the value, and convert it into cash or gold or bonds. But, after a while, they are back again. Busy buying the bull market. Why? Because a bull market is still the best place to grow money.

Time and again the investors perceive a threat and sell their holdings. Now, the sale could be for any reason. It could be because of bad policy announcement, or a missed earnings estimate, or a bad crop season, or perhaps the threat of an impending war or virus. The investors, for all their investment power, can only sell their holdings and buy them back later. Whenever a few large investors sell and depress the market a bit, more investors join in. This is a flight response because of herd mentality. It triggers when there is a perception of threat and amplifies when everyone else around is behaving in the same way.

However, there is a key difference between the situation of the pigeons and the investors. While the flight response of the pigeon saves their lives, the flight response of the investors gives them sub-optimal results (or at times destroys their capital). This is because, in the physical world of the pigeons, the threat is real, confirmed, and with dire consequences. On the contrary, in the imagined reality of the markets, the threat is only as much as it is perceived by the investor. The response is clearly irrational, yet highly predictable. This is because of how investor portfolios are constructed, concentrated in one asset class, and cornered to a few instruments.

If an investor's portfolio is well-diversified and still contains a few bad bets, she need not worry. The good portion of the portfolio can take care of the bad parts in turbulent times. However, most portfolios we come across are not well diversified either in terms of the number of holdings or in terms of the underlying asset classes. Neither is there any insurance on such portfolios. Such portfolios are the reason for great pride when the times are good and a source of great stress when the markets are bad. Ideally, asset allocation has to be as per the risk capacity, not as per your risk preferences.

Profiting From Predictable Irrationality

In order to profit from this behaviour, we can use a simple strategy. It is something which is available as conventional wisdom but needs some well-defined parameters to execute. Conventional wisdom says that in a bull market (of equity, commodity, currency, etc) you should

"buy on dips".

That is about it. However, a few things that need to be ascertained before this is done. Firstly, you should be able to determine whether it's a bull market or not. In a bull market, prices go up most of the time but the pace is slow. Technical chartists describe it as higher highs mostly and higher lows. This is the easiest way to identify. You will get a lot of noise from the news about the impending build-up of doom. You will need to filter it and keep focus on the bigger picture. An advisor or a professional money manager can help with this.

Next, you need to define what a dip is. There are many definitions of a dip. It is called a sell-off, profit-taking, a correction. However, if not defined in simple mathematical terms, it can cause you to panic. An easy way to identify a dip is the market trading below the 200-day moving average (200 DMA). This is a widely cited measurement and is available on many websites and channels. So the strategy is that in a bull market, buy below the 200 DMA. This is a good zone to buy. However, there is still one more challenge to overcome.

Below the 200 DMA, you will have to overcome your flight response and actually buy. In terms of birds, you will have to be the crow who easily hops in and pecks its stomach full with the best grains when the pigeons are circling around. The crow carefully observes the pigeons from atop its perch and tracks the threats. As soon as the pigeons are threatened, the crow swoops down and feasts itself. In short, the crow behaves contrarian. Similarly, threats in a bull market are opportunities to enter. It is a classic case of price versus value mismatch and keeping it cool to be able to find it. Easy for us to write here yet difficult to implement for us too.

The final component of the strategy to profit from irrationality is to have some cash to buy. If the markets fall and you find abundant good prices to enter, you can only enter when you have some cash. Mostly everyone is always fully invested. It means the crow must stay hungry in order to feast on the best grains when available. Otherwise, it will be full of the bad stuff it ate earlier.

If you are fully invested with no spare cash, the good stuff will come, you will smile and say no thank you. So the final step to profit from predictable irrationality is to always have some cash spared. This can be done in many ways, one of which is dynamic asset allocation. Again, it is recommended that you take the advice of an investment advisor or fund manager to execute such strategies.

Chapter 13

---◆---

500 Points Movement

A Five Hundred Point Movement on the NIFTY 50 Index

Sameer had started his career in finance in 2007. It was the peak of the bull market. Little did he know that he would learn so much in the coming two years. The market was at its volatile best and moved aggressively both downwards and upwards. For a professional working in equity risk management, the global financial crisis, which saw markets across the globe correct by more than 60%, was a testing time.

The theories and methodologies Sameer had learnt were put to test, stretched, and checked for exceptions. Some of what he had learnt in his CFA course stood good, yet a lot of it did not. However, the news which reflected the human perspective of this movement only saw it as excitement and anxiety. The market was always moving some points up or down. The reasons ascribed are varied, but the buzz was not.

On 18 May 2009, the NIFTY50 index opened at 3673.15. Immediately after opening, the market started moving upwards at a very fast pace. The movement upwards was so fast that there was a trading halt or "freeze". The trading resumed and the market moved wildly up again. By the end of the day, the NIFTY50 index had moved 651.50 points from the previous day's close to finish at 4323.15. The intra-day movement itself was 711.15 points. A whopping 17.74% change in a single day. The reason ascribed to this exuberance was the re-election of the incumbent government. It was as if the entire economy of India was just dependent on this one thing.

Fast-forward to 2019. On September 20, 2019, the markets were sluggish while opening in the morning. There were talks of a recession at hand. The mood on social media was gloomy and so were the newspapers and channels. Everyone was cursing the government for its lack of action and lagging policy. Around 11 a.m, the finance minister of India addressed a press conference and announced a tax break for certain types of corporations. The change in the stance of the government was unexpected and sudden. Perceiving this move as positive, the market reacted and started to move up. By the closing bell, the movement was 569.40 points to finish at 11274.20. However, there was no freeze because the movement was merely 5.32% in a day. A large move nonetheless.

The media again was excited and published that this was by far the biggest movement in a certain time frame. A 500 point plus move in the nation's flagship Large Cap index was something to be celebrated and awed at. The news headline said, "The NIFTY moved more than five hundred points in a single trading session today!" on both days in 2009 and 2019. In the year 2009, it meant the index moved by a whopping 17%. In the year 2019, it meant about 5%. 10 years later, when the NIFTY50 index is (hopefully) at 25,000, it would mean only 2%. Even though the percentage move is very different, the news always prints it as 500 points.

Our minds are designed to note a 500 point movement. We cannot help it. It is by design. The news is engineered around this design of the mind. The media will always dramatize the headline. Yet the consequences of these 500 points are very different. In one case it meant being wiped out or creating a fortune depending on whether you were leveraged and were short or long respectively. In the second case, it meant a significant loss but manageable if you reversed a short position.

The Consequence of the Denominator

An intra-day 500 point movement has happened only a few times in the NIFTY50 index over the last 12 years. As the value of the index grows, it will keep happening more and more often, until it becomes too insignificant to be reported by the media (as it has happened with the SENSEX). Let us not blame the news, the human mind has a genuine difficulty in calculating and understanding percentage points. So it sticks to the easier thing to notice, the absolute number or points.

Points are easier to compute, talk about, and remember. They only involve simple arithmetic and are unique, unlike percentages which are the same 1 to 100. This is called the framing effect in Behavioural psychology. The framing effect addresses how a reference point, oftentimes a meaningless benchmark, when presented, can affect our decision making by creating a comparison. We are naturally inclined towards comparisons of absolutes. The media knows this too and reports the way it does, for our convenience. Points are the proxy developed by the human perspective for the more difficult percentages which are meaningful but represent the financial perspective.

However, you should not act upon the points movement (seasoned market professionals never do). The drama associated with a large point movement is entirely up to us. This is because we have a memory which fixates us to a figure. This behavioural bias is called the anchoring effect, where an individual depends too heavily on an initial piece of information offered to make subsequent judgments during decision making. Once the value of this anchor is set, all future negotiations, arguments, estimates, etc. are discussed in relation to the anchor.

This fixation and its dramatization can be managed easily by comparing the number to another number, typically by finding a relevant denominator. Hans Rosling explains this technique in his book *Factfulness*. It is important to do this because it leads to better decisions by creating a comparison. Markets are not an absolute of today, they are a relative to yesterday, the week before, a month, or a few years ago.

As an investor in the markets, doing the comparison exercise will set you apart. It will tell you what is of consequence and what is not and you can formulate strategies to profit from it. Markets will move in jumps of 500 points or more many times. These moves will seldom be predictable. However, putting the move into perspective with a denominator makes all the difference in what is to be done then or later.

The Second Thing About a 500 Point Movement

Whenever markets move 500 points up i.e., a significant move in a day with respect to the preceding days, there is denial. Investors simply refuse to believe that the event has happened. They continue their previous stance and escalate their commitment. This means that an investor who had a bearish stance (no long positions or short positions because they felt the market will go down) continues to stay bearish even after the event's shock.

We have further observed that in their shock, investors increase their positions against the market. They feel they have to be redeemed for the wrongdoing done to them because of the shock. As a result, they suffer more losses as the market moves against them. More money is lost in the days succeeding a 500 point movement than on the day of the movement. It could be because of the covering of positions against the market or perhaps just the complete assimilation of information or perhaps any other reason. We do not know. There is little research pointing to the reasons, but it mostly happens. Interestingly, the media always comes up with an explanation which seems obvious later.

Profiting from Large Moves

The simplest strategy to profit from large market moves is to follow the direction of the move. This is true when the move is in the positive direction and the market is already depressed badly (near 52-week lows), or in the negative direction when the market was exalted (near all-time high). Let's call this strategy "playing with the move".

On the contrary, if the move is upwards, when the market is exalted, or downwards when the market is beaten, then there is likely going to be a reversal. The playing against the move strategy is contrarian in nature. This is a more risky bet than the playing with the move strategy.

The trick here is to know where the market stands when the large move happens. Contrastingly, most investors are focussed on predicting the large moves, whereas the money is made in the aftermath of the move. Refer to Table 8 on how to act after a large move, but with money management rules in place.

Table 8: Profiting from a Large Move

	Market Exalted	**Market Depressed**
Large Move UP	Play against the Move.	Play with the Move.
Large Move DOWN	Play with the Move.	Play against the Move.

Large moves happen, the media always reports it with excitement, investors deny the consequence and the reasons are unknown. The smarter thing is to know what happened, acknowledge it, and act upon it rather than trying to predict when it will happen.

Chapter 14

Luck, Skill, and Randomness

Luck or Skill

Sameer's friend from school, Karan, runs his family business which supplies electrical inverters. He and his father run the shop from Janakpuri. The business is good, but has only enough work to involve Karan and his father. Karan has a younger brother, Varun. Varun was always good at studies and his father figured that his younger son should study abroad and get a good job. He wanted Varun to settle abroad. However, by the time Varun had graduated in 2011, there were few jobs available. So, Varun came back to India and started working in an MNC.

One day, in June of 2014, Karan called up Sameer and told him that he wanted him to guide his younger brother on career options in the stock market. He told Sameer that Varun had quit his job after 1 year and was now sitting at home, adamant on making stock trading his full-time profession. He also told Sameer that Varun had made some money in the stock markets over the past 3 years. The boy was now sitting on the money and was awestruck with his talent in the markets. Karan wanted Sameer to guide his brother for a possible career in the markets. Sameer agreed and invited Varun to chat over a coffee.

The two met over coffee. Sameer asked Varun how he had managed to amass a superb return from the markets, being so young and inexperienced. Varun told Sameer that he had invested all his salary in the best stocks and now he was getting good returns. This was because he was skilled at stock picking. Listening to Varun's reply, he was not surprised by the answer. On investigating further about these investments, Sameer learnt that these investments were made in December of 2011.

Role of Randomness

Serendipity often masquerades as skill. The top three investing skills are patience, temperament, and having your investment coincide with an uninterrupted bull run or a chronological lottery. December 2011 was a time when the Indian stock markets were bottoming out. It was a time of low sentiment. At that time, if anyone had bought small caps and mid caps, they would have made a fortune by May of 2014. Sameer understood that this was sheer beginners luck. Yet, he was unable to translate the reason for Varun's success to him. Varun was convinced that it was his skill, and skill alone that had bought him this success.

Human beings have evolved to seek and know the reason behind events happening around them. This helps them to form a cogent model of reality around themselves. The models help us establish a cause and effect relationship between events and outcomes. It is how we learn. This model is essential for our survival.

In the physical world, the cause and effect relationships always holds true. For example, if you try putting your hand in fire, you will immediately learn that your hand burns and hurts. Similarly, if you add just the right amount of sugar to your coffee, it will be pleasingly sweet. A little more and the coffee becomes unpalatable.

While negative experiences (like putting your hand in fire) teach us what not to do in the very first go, positive experiences (the right amount of sugar) need a few tries to get just right. Which means you have practised adding sugar to your coffee many times to know now how much is good for your taste.

Cause and effect relationships are always true in the physical world. Their predictability is almost certain. So we observe the predictability and form the laws of physics. It helps make life simple and safe.

However, the cause and effect relationship model is so hardcoded in the brain that we unknowingly and erroneously extend it to the happenings in the conceptual world as well. When markets move up or down, we try to find reasons and fit explanations to the moves.

Markets are not like the physical world. They behave predictably most of the time, and misbehave randomly at other times, or become highly irrational for certain periods. The markets may be headed in a certain direction and then, randomly, may reverse the direction. These changes in direction often result in reactions which seriously affect investor portfolios, negatively or positively. From an investor's perspective who loses money, it is called bad luck. For the one who makes money, it is lauded as a skill. In psychology, this is called internalizing success and externalizing failure or commonly known as the self-serving bias, a cognitive or perceptual process that is distorted by the need to maintain and enhance self-esteem. This is how humans explain randomness and its consequences to themselves.

BullC**p after a Bullrun

After every bull run, a lot of investors ask us about if they should quit their jobs to become full-time investors in the stock market. Many people want to do this because they think they have a "knack for finding potential multi-baggers," or to use a term very popular these days, a "knack for identifying emerging moats." However, such thoughts are often masked by survivorship bias, which is an error of concentrating only on people or things that "survived" some process and inadvertently overlooking those who failed and faded away.

Nassim Taleb, in his book *Fooled by Randomness*, talks exactly about "luck disguised and perceived as non-luck (that is, skills) and, more generally, randomness disguised and perceived as non-randomness (that is, determinism)." He goes on to say, *"Don't mistake luck for skill."*

"There is one world in which I believe the habit of mistaking luck for skill is most prevalent – and most conspicuous – and that is the world of markets ... we often have the mistaken impression that a strategy is an excellent strategy, or an entrepreneur a person endowed with "vision," or a trader a talented trader, only to realize that 99.9% of their past performance is attributable to chance, and chance alone. Ask a profitable investor to explain the reasons for his success; he will offer some deep and convincing interpretation of the results. Frequently, these delusions are intentional and deserve to bear the name charlatanism."

A common folly of assuming we are skilful, when we are actually just plain lucky, is in our tendency to think it's easy to be a successful investor. The vulnerability to this error is magnified especially during a successful bull market. The ultra-successful investors are few, but their stories have an outsized effect on us. We believe we can succeed because they did. The world of investing produces success stories and failures. It's human nature to wish to copy success. However, an ironic truth is this: To accept success, and especially quick success at face value, without acknowledging the role of luck is a strategy for failure. So, taking inspiration from other full-time investors who have made good money from "emerging moats" or "penny stocks" or "value trading", and ignoring others who followed similar processes but ended up with disasters can lead you to false conclusions about your own potential as a full-time investor.

You have to understand that investing is not to make you rich, but it is a way to keep you rich and help you grow your purchasing power. What makes you rich is always your efforts which increases your cycle income and the compounding of your cycle profits by putting them back into investments as discussed in the personal finance cycle in chapter 2. It's the earning from your work, and what you do with it, that will make you rich along with focussing on the right inefficiencies of the cycle. Plus a lot of good luck!

GOBC

Being lucky and mistaking it for skill is what Varun experienced. Varun's entering the stock markets at a low point was purely chance. Further, the run from December 2011 to May 2014 was also not his doing. It was simply the markets running up. Varun's fortune in his investing activities was purely luck. But Varun is a human being. He needs to explain things to himself. He observes like all other humans, forms a hypothesis, tests it, and then comes to a conclusion. His inexperience gets the better of him. The human perspective ends up explaining complex things with simple explanations and attributes simplistic reasons to these happenings. It is a pure case of GOBC (Good Observation, Bad Conclusion).

Play Money Portfolio

Most "would-be talented stock investors" have not experienced a Black Swan event or bear market in equities. They have not seen their capital eroded by 60-70%. Few survive to tell the tale and invest during a bear phase because the valuation was now right. This essentially means they have not faced volatility or experienced the gut-wrenching pain of having your life's savings evaporate (and remain so for the next 12 to 18 months). We always tell them, "If you have also not experienced the downfall, please don't get down to full-time investing before you gain this experience."

In fact, if you seriously want to get down to becoming a full-time investor, first learn how to do it sensibly, test your skills (by investing part of your savings in stocks), and go through the volatile market cycles before making a decision. It always makes sense to have a play money portfolio. Such a portfolio should not be more than 10% of your investments. The rest should be given to professional management.

Which Skills to Pay for?

Like Varun, we are all susceptible to bad conclusions. Only experience can rectify these conclusions. The better strategy is to hire a money manager and pay for their skills to make money for you.

You win by default when you do not do stupid things. As an investor, you should remember that markets are random and unpredictable. Short term success is not skill. So you should choose a money manager who knows how their returns came. Good managers do not focus on picking winners, they focus on rejecting losers. This is called Via negativa (The art of saying NO - subtract, subtract, subtract).

Winners are a product of randomness, no one can really predict them. Instead, a good money manager focuses on not doing things that are known to lose money. The trend takes care of the wins. A good manager knows that getting super-normal returns from the market is a bonus, not their skill. It is luck and an experienced market professional always thanks his luck. They do not blame bad results on luck or attribute good results to their skills. In fact, they do the reverse. As an investor, you should remember that bad results are due to lack of skill and good results are because of luck.

The table below will give you an indication of what real money-making skills (for the long term) are versus what is perceived as money-making skills. The list is not exhaustive, but we hope you understand the role of randomness and differentiating the type of skills and luck. Knowing which skill to pay for is your job as an investor. Executing the skill is the fund manager's job. It is best not to mix up! Table 9 sums up the difference between the perceived skill and actual skill in specific areas.

Table 9: Which Skills to pay for

Area	Perceived Skills	Actual Skills
Market Timing	Predicting tops and bottoms accurately.	Dynamic Asset Allocation - Knowing how much exposure to take to a certain asset.
Asset Allocation	Knowing how to choose & time the winning asset class.	Finding complementing asset classes having varying cycles.
Portfolio Construction	Picking winning stock.	Constructing diversified portfolios which are goal-oriented.
Performance	Maximizing returns.	Optimizing risks exposure.
Diversification	Statistical diversification of stocks in a portfolio to have a minimal correlation.	Risk diversification of assets in a portfolio to minimize concurrent shocks in multiple asset classes with respect to your financial goals.
Stock Picking	Picking winners	Eliminating losers

Chapter 15

Everything has a Purpose

The Red Fruit

Myra is growing up. She has started playschool and is learning new things fast. The adorable, almost four-year-old can sing up to four poems along with the dance moves, count till 10, and identify colours with some consistency. On an election holiday in Maharashtra, the exchanges are closed and Sameer is home. Myra's playschool is on. The school finishes at 12 p.m and Sameer picks her up. On the way back, Myra is excited to see that she will be riding with papa. Sameer boards her into the car. As they drive on, he asks Myra how was her day and what did she learn. Myra, the cute chatterbox, tells papa all about the day and what she learned. They reach home 30 minutes later and Myra is already hungry. Priya senses her child's need and brings out a bowl of fruit on the dining table. She asks Myra which one she will have. To this question, the innocent child replies, "The red fruit." Priya asks which one, the apple or the pomegranate. Myra points to the apple. Priya gets busy peeling and slicing the apple.

Across the room, Sameer observes the choice Myra made and how she communicated it. He figures that Myra has been learning about colours in the playschool. To her, the fruits are red or orange or yellow, not apples and pomegranate or oranges or bananas. It is easier for Myra to recall the fruits by their colour attribute than by their names because the names are more complex. However, the two red fruits are very different in taste, structure, the way they are consumed and even their effects on the stomach later. Myra simply calls the fruit with its name which is its most striking attribute: colour. In doing so, she simplifies the name to the easiest thing to remember.

For us grown-ups in the world of investing, we too box various types of investments by their simplest attribute i.e., asset class. Gold is the best example here. Gold comes in the form of jewellery, or in the form of coins and bars, or in electronic form like an ETF or a mutual fund, or even in the form of sovereign gold bonds. Each of these instruments is backed by some form of gold. However, their characteristics differ a lot when it comes to the use of an individual. Gold bonds, for example, pay an interest of about 2.5% and have a lock-in for taxation purposes. However, they are also relatively illiquid in comparison to gold mutual funds or ETFs which can be sold in a jiffy. Similarly, gold jewellery has making charges associated with it and is less liquid than gold bars or coins. However, gold jewellery has an ornamental use too which the gold bars and coins do not have.

Despite all these differences, investors (including all of us) still club gold as a single asset class when constructing our portfolios. This makes our portfolios much different in its characteristics than that for the intended purpose.

Defining Purpose

In little Myra's world, there are no such things as investments or stock markets or currencies or bonds or debentures or commodities. Neither are there any brokers, asset management companies, or stock exchanges. There is nothing in her imagination called a financial institution or even money. These are all concepts adults have and discuss between them. All of these concepts are constructs of adult human minds. Nevertheless, these constructs are important because they make Myra's world function as well.

All of these constructs are executed and homogenized through contracts adults have in between them and are bound to agree upon. These contracts have specific characteristics and are called financial instruments. Every financial instrument has a purpose, either singular or multiple. Every asset class, whether debt or equity or gold or real estate or anything else, needs an instrument. The financial instrument allows the investor to execute a transaction, have ownership of the asset, and benefit from it in some form. Along with these properties, each financial instrument has more attributes attached to it, which gives it certain characteristics such as periodic payouts (in the form of dividends or interest), guarantees, or other contractual obligations.

Financial instruments are supposed to serve our needs. Yet, we end up spending a lot of effort in meeting the contractual obligations of the financial instrument and wondering how its features would work. The trick is to quickly and effectively decode the essential features of an instrument from a viewpoint of the individuals' needs. Rather than approaching from the financial perspective, (as done traditionally), an approach from the human perspective serves better to classify and select various instruments.

The Three Essential Investor Needs from the Human Perspective

We primarily have 3 essential needs when it comes to investing. We need money for present consumption, future consumption, and a buffer to cover the unexpected.

Present consumption entails the money required for day to day living. The time frame for this spending of money is immediate or in the near future up to 3 to 6 months time. From this definition, kitchen and household expenses, transportation, rent, and EMI, fees, personal maintenance, etc. all fall under present consumption. Present consumption invariably becomes a fixed cost per month and varies only a bit from month to month. This cost may increase on an annual basis owing to inflation or change in lifestyle.

When we aspire for goals or perceive a need for money in the distant future, then we are essentially planning for future consumption. The typical time frame for this type of money spending is more than 6 months and, at most times, can be as long as several years.

Future consumption targets can be saving for retirement, education of children or self, purchasing a house, building a corpus to start a business, planning a vacation etc. For such targets, we need to save money and invest it as well to grow it. Future consumption targets are essentially known in advance (accurately or as an estimation) and are planned.

Yet, at times, our lives do not always go as planned. There can be negative events which we cannot plan for. Such negative events are not always completely unknown and can be documented from others' lives. Examples of such negative events, which can be planned to be covered for, are the death of an earning member, loss because of theft, fire or natural disaster, etc., a stock market crash leading to portfolio value loss, and many more. Negative events can happen to either a single individual (tragedy) or to everyone as a collective (Black Swan event, discussed in a later chapter). Therefore, creating a buffer is an essential human requirement. This buffer comes useful in times of crisis.

Given these needs, we can understand any financial instrument and quickly comprehend if it is fit for us or not and whether it should be part of our portfolio. However, investors still end up misusing financial instruments by doing the wrong things with them. Some misuse cases are discussed below.

Misuse Case: Using Equity for Present Consumption or Buffer

Equity is primarily an instrument serving future consumption. It is designed to grow in value over time as the underlying company's business and profits grow. When times are bad, the valuation of the company may fall as well. The company which ordinarily gives dividends (say every quarter) may not give these dividends (or give lesser amounts) during these times. This is because the company may now tap into its excess cash reserves to bolster its lagging operations. In another scenario, the company may decide to enter a new field and use the excess cash it has, to fund this new growth. In this case, too, it will not give the desired dividends.

In both scenarios, individuals who are banking upon the company to give dividends for funding their present consumption will be left short of their needs. Using stock dividends to fund present consumption is a poor use of equity.

Similarly, a stock portfolio cannot be used to cover an exigent circumstance like death of the primary earner in a family. The stock portfolio fluctuates with the market conditions. In the case of an exigent circumstance, the stock portfolio may not be able to provide as much value to the family because of poor market conditions, such as a recession or a correction phase. In such a case, a life insurance cover would suit better. It would provide a known amount of corpus to the family. The stock portfolio, in this case, would not be immediately used for present consumption and the family can wait to redeem it at a more opportune time when the market conditions are favourable.

Misuse Case: Using Fixed Income for Future Consumption

Fixed income, as the name suggests, is intended to provide a payout at regular intervals. However, it is often used to compound money by taking risks. A prime example of this is low credit quality bonds. These bonds do provide higher rates of return while they are in a good market scenario. However, they default more often than expected. This is a factor overlooked by individuals when considering them for investment. The individuals could simply invest in equity for longer terms in order to get higher returns.

Making a Soup

Priya is a good cook. She was always interested in culinary skills and often followed cooking shows on TV. With these shows, she learnt how to get innovative with food. One area of interest for her is soups. Making soups permits her to bring a wide variety of flavours together in one sip. As complex as they seem, good soups are really simple to make. You just have to not mix the wrong things together.

Mixing old ingredients to form new flavours is a great art. However, it is best left experimenting with food. In the world of investing, mixing flavours lead to bad tasting outcomes. Most people would not mix lemons with milk to make a soup. This is because everyone understands that these flavours do not mix well and end up making the soup sour.

Yet bad instruments with complex investing outcomes keep on continuing to be served to investors for years and years together. This is because of mass marketing and mis-selling or the lack of simple innovative solutions or the lack of effort of investors to educate themselves about these products or a combination of these. The result has been a bad taste.

Complex Instruments

If a financial instrument tries to serve more than one function in a significant manner, then we can call it a complex instrument. This means that if an instrument tries to serve future consumption as well as act as a buffer at the same time (or any other combination), we can classify it as a complex instrument. For example, a unit linked insurance plan (ULIP) which provides growth in the form of market exposure and tax saving (increment), and also provides life cover of a minimum value (insurance), then we can classify it as a complex instrument. We would like to give a disclaimer here that we too have been the victims of complex instruments.

By the above definition, if an instrument does provide more than 1 function but the extra functions do not significantly change the functioning of the instrument, then it is a simple instrument. For example, an equity stock which grows in value despite giving dividends from time to time (which can be reinvested as well) is a simple instrument. This is because the dividends are of less significance in character than the growth of the stock's value.

Reason for the Existence of Complex Instruments

Complex instruments exist because they provide convenience to individuals owning them by serving the human perspective in the short run. This convenience means individuals have to expend less time and effort themselves to create a portfolio which serves multiple needs. This effort is done by someone else i.e., the issuers of the complex instrument. The need is called oversimplification.

Complexity is expensive. Whenever issuers of a complex instrument provide convenience, they charge a fee for it. This fee can be explicit in the form of a charge or implicit in the form of misaligned incentives like upfront commission which leads to poor performance.

We also come across investors who get emotionally worked up and end up with these instruments. Consequently, they find themselves with exceedingly complicated portfolios.

We believe that instruments should be simple and portfolios should be sophisticated. Yet there are countless numbers of instruments which are complex and portfolios which are complicated. When purposes get mixed up, explosive situations and long term traps are created. Here are a few examples where complex instruments are soups of the wrong flavours put together.

ULIPS or Unit Linked Insurance Plans

These instruments try to provide life insurance, capital protection, market returns, and tax-saving together. ULIPs turn out to be expensive instruments to participate in the markets. Their costing structure gives insurance coverage at a very high price by charging a higher mortality premium than pure term-insurance policies. Investors are neither left with good returns nor do they get optimal insurance coverage.

Hybrid Funds

These instruments try to mix debt and equity in some proportions and thereby try to give a balanced portfolio. Rules around hybrid funds make them less nimble to respond to market cycles of different underlying instruments. They also end up taking a higher risk in debt in an effort to generate alpha to compensate for the lesser exposure to equity. The underlying mix of instruments of a hybrid fund can be emulated at a much lower cost and with a more efficient asset allocation as well.

Deep Discount Bonds

These instruments try to give equity-like perpetuity to debt and intend to return value over the long term (25 to 30 years). Often such commitments tend to fall short after a few years and there is a permanent loss of capital or a sub-par return unless they are sovereign issued and guaranteed. There are famous examples when semi-government issuers of such bonds retired them mid-term and left the investors' hopes thwarted along with long-pending litigation.

Retirement Plans and Pension Schemes

Pension schemes give tax-saving and market returns. By their design, pension schemes give a payout at the retirement age. Most pension schemes are market-linked and do pay out significantly less when the market has fallen at the time of the payout. You may delay the payout by a few years hoping for the recovery of the markets but you may have to stay poor for those years.

Children Plans

These plans have long term commitments and contain penalties which end up paying sub-par returns. The supposed benefit is tax saving but the rules are complicated. Typically, the end payout figures seem very nice. However, when adjusted for inflation, the returns are only ordinary.

Avoiding complexity is an area where the financial perspective overrides the human perspective in the short run so as to better serve the human perspective in the longer run. This implies that while a complex instrument does provide the apparent convenience of less effort in the short run, this convenience comes at a heavy cost.

Detecting and Avoiding Complexity

The following signs are an indication of a complex instrument.

1. There is a lock-in period longer than 3 years.
2. There are a variety of upfront charges which recur.
3. The instrument appeals to our convenience of not having many accounts or engaging many instruments.
4. The instrument appeals to our emotional biases and uses language which involves talking about the future and the possibility of negative eventualities for us and our loved ones. Typically talking about our parents, children, or spouses.
5. The instrument talks about downside protection and good returns at the same time eg., *"Growth bhi aur protection bhi."*

If the significant functions of the instrument can be exactly replicated by a combination of 2 or more simple instruments, then the complex instrument should be avoided (at all costs!). The financial cost of using a complex instrument is higher than the cognitive cost of constructing the same features using simple instruments.

There are a host of unsavoury soups of instruments available out there. Their primary ingredients are:

- Tax-saving features
- Long term lock-ins
- Supposed convenience or peace of mind
- An emotional appeal to your future self or to the future of your loved ones

As an investor, your aim should be to find simple instruments and avoid complex ones. Complex instruments have hidden costs and are susceptible to systematic shocks. That is why it has been said:

"Keep it simple."

PART 4

What My MBA Did Not Teach Me About ME

Chapter 16

---◆---

We are Designed to React

Flight Crisis

It's December, the time for the annual family holiday. This year Sameer and Sumit, along with Priya, Poorni, and Myra have decided to go to Goa for a vacation. All five have already boarded the flight from Mumbai to Goa. The excitement is high. Poorni loves Goa and it's Priya's first trip to the beach capital of India as well. The boys, Sameer and Sumit, have plans to hire a car and explore the countryside and spend evenings on the beach. All is settled with the hotel bookings and entertainment planned.

The announcements are made and the pilot of the flight is Captain Suraj Rathi. Captain Rathi has recently been promoted to take command. With only about 100 hours of flying as Captain and 3000 plus hours in total, he is new to being responsible for the entire flight. His co-pilot and First Officer is Debina Roy, a relatively new pilot with about 500 hours of flying experience in total. It is a bright sunny day in Mumbai, with slight crosswinds. The flight is ready and taxis down the runway. Shortly, the ATC gives the clear signal to take off. Captain Rathi is off with the twin-engine plane. He makes a good clean take off. The instruction to fly is at FL350 or 35,000 ft. After the take-off, the ascent is steady. In the passenger area, seat belt signs are on and everyone is calm.

At 20,000 feet there is a loud boom. The starboard (right) engine starts to exhaust flames. A passenger looks outside the window and screams fire! The flight attendant immediately senses the panic and gets off her seat. As she moves down the aisle, another long boom comes. The engine screams aloud and catches fire.

Inside the cabin, the gauges on Captain Rathi's heads up display are dropping. He immediately senses the fault. Next up, he sees that the temperature of the starboard engine is rising. He quickly calls to his co-pilot, Debina, and instructs her to pull the QRH - (Quick Reference Handbook). Debina is puzzled and frozen. The captain looks at her and tells her to react. Fortunately, she snaps out of her freeze and asks him for the instructions again. The captain tells her to pull out the page for engine failure. The QRH contains the detailed instructions of the procedure to be followed in such a situation. She fumbles and pulls out the wrong page and starts to read out. The captain senses her error and tells her, "Okay! I have coms and control. Hand me over the QRH." As he takes the QRH, he pulls out the right page and starts to follow the instructions. He cuts the fuel line to the starboard engine, and halts the ascent, stabilizing the plane at 22,000 feet.

Next, he opens the channel and shouts, "Mayday, mayday, mayday." The ATC Mumbai immediately responds and asks about the problem. Captain Rathi responds that he has an engine failure and requests a flyback. He further tells them to standby.

Meanwhile, the head crew calls him from the cabin. She reports to him anxiously that the left engine is on fire. Captain Rathi quickly checks his gauges. He sees that the right engine is not responding. Captain Rathi realizes that if the left engine has failed and he has stopped the right engine then the flight is doomed. He quickly asks the crew to re-check the status and says his instrument shows the starboard or the right engine has trouble.

All this time, the BlackBox recorder is noting the status, the actions and conversations. Captain Rathi has to get a visual confirmation from the head crew. The crew's back is towards the cockpit. She sees the engine on her left, but for the plane, it is the one on the right. She quickly realizes her error and reports that it is the right engine that has failed. The captain sighs with relief. She further reports that the engine is no longer on fire but is breathing smoke into the cabin.

The passengers sense the plane's descent and see the smoke in the cabin. They are in a panic already. Priya is tightly hugging Myra and Poorni is clenching Sumit's arm. Sameer is pushing his hands against the front seat with his eyes shut tightly.

Smoke. Captain Rathi now understands that he has to not only stabilize the plane but also eject the smoke. If he only safely lands the plane, the smoke will most likely kill the passengers by then. He senses that since the engine is shut the smoke should subside, else he will have to follow the procedure for ejecting the smoke. The plane is now at 15,000 feet. It will be a few thousand more feet before he can start ejecting the smoke. As he descends the plane further, he asks the crew about the status of the smoke. Fortunately, she responds that the smoke has subsided. Good news! Captain Rathi radios the ATC for an emergency landing. The ATC tells him to standby. A minute later the ATC responds that he has a clear runway to land.

Eight minutes later, Captain Rathi lands the plane. The fire is out, and the left engine is still running. He decides to go to "Pan-Pan" status and requests the ATC to allow taxiing the plane to a dock. He gets a green signal and safely docks the plane 10 minutes later.

Sameer, Sumit, and the family safely deboard the plane along with all the other passengers. More than a hundred lives were saved. The plane is flooded with flight engineers and technicians. Fifteen minutes later, the captain also deboards the plane, after answering a plethora of questions from the ground team. He gets an ovation from the crew and the passengers.

We React by Design

With only 100 hours as captain, and never having faced a similar situation in his flying career, Captain Rathi still managed to save the day. Was it his experience that helped or was it a combination of something else?

We are not designed to calculate risk. We do not analyze the situation in real-time and act accordingly. We are designed to react immediately. Why? Because our ancestors, who lived in Savannah, did not have time to assess their odds when they were being charged by a lion. They just ran for their lives. The reaction was inbuilt. It meant survival. The survival instincts from then are still there within us now. They protect us from physical and emotional harm.

In the modern day, when we see trouble in any situation, we react. Captain Rathi reacted too when he sensed trouble. However, he controlled his first reaction through his training. He did not respond in the way any ordinary person would, with fear, and he did not become paralyzed. Instead, he reacted with what he was trained to do. His first reaction was to cut the fuel supply to the engine. These were the only steps he needed to remember.

After identifying the problem and getting on top of the situation, he did not act any further on his own. Instead, after that, he pulled out the QRH and followed the checklist or algorithm. Step-by-step he took control of the situation and he shaped the result with only the skills he had already been trained for: flying on a single engine and landing. Not even for one moment did he feel heroic and tried to handle the situation in his own way.

All of us also react to bad news in the markets with respect to our investments. We do not assess or compute an effective strategy to neutralize the risk. Our brain does not work that way. We react. In fact, by the time you would have computed an effective strategy to compensate for an event hurting your portfolio, everyone else would have already reacted and sold their holdings. The price would be down and you would end up being in a greater panic. By the time you finally give in and decide to sell, it would probably be a good time to buy (and you will only acknowledge that in hindsight).

Instead, the only thing that is required for us to do when trouble hits our portfolio is to follow a plan. This plan is a checklist or an algorithm. While Captain Rathi had very little time to control his reaction and pull out his QRH, it is not the same for us with investments.

There is nothing immediately needed to be done within seconds when the market starts to go down. The urge does come by, but nothing really needs to be done immediately. The urgency instinct cannot be suppressed. However, it can be directed. There is not enough time to compute the optimum reaction, so a plan or a step by step checklist is very important to be put in place in advance.

Reactive Advice

"The time to be defensive is not during the crisis, but before the crisis."

Unfortunately, most advice around investing only tells you what you should have not done when there was trouble. It tells you that you should not have reacted in that particular way. However, we know that it is very difficult not to react because we are designed to do so. We do not blame such reactive advice. Many advice givers have not been around long enough to know that the market for any asset (be it stocks, bonds, real estate, or even cryptocurrencies) follows a cycle of troubles and celebrations.

Similar to flying in airplanes, the majority of all the troubling situations have already happened before and are documented. The reasons and mechanics might be different each time, but the situation is the same. The pilots do not get highly paid for just the flying. They get paid for years of training on how to handle a crisis and control the first reaction, so that they can be on top of the situation. Financial memory, on the other hand, is very short. Casualties of one market cycle do not stay around to pass over the lessons to the next set of investors. However, there are plenty of plans available on how to be on top of a financial situation. It is just a matter of knowing and following these plans.

The Investor and the Good Financial Advisor

A good financial advisor will always have a plan to handle a troubled situation in the markets. A good financial advisor will know your shortcomings and have a plan to shield you from your own reactions in times of turbulence. He will know that your mind (and his own) will react sharply to bad news and will act upon it in a state of panic. To tackle this, he will have a plan and a checklist ready. A good financial advisor does not manage the investors' money but instead guides the investor's behaviour or reaction, and the money manages itself.

The good advisor also knows that you are likely to pick up the right advice for the wrong situation. For example, there is an old adage in investing which says,

> *"Cut short your losses and let your winners run."*

This is great advice for a bull market. However, this advice does not hold true when the market has already fallen. The losses in your portfolio, when the entire market falls, are not losses, they are depressed values. Booking losses at depressed values and staying out of the market leads to a permanent loss of capital.

In fact, depressed values are opportunities to buy. A good financial advisor knows this. Therefore, instead of telling you what to do when the market has already fallen, he would have already prepared an action plan in advance. This plan will tell you, step-by-step, what to do when an exigent event happens. As a part of the plan, he will allocate part of your funds to cash, so that fresh purchases can be made as well. He might make you shift to a portfolio which has a faster chance of recovery by dynamically managing asset allocation based on years to your goals.

The Great Financial Advisor

A great financial advisor, on the other hand, would completely bypass the troubled times. His challenge would be to negotiate with you to sell when everyone else would be in a buying frenzy and vice-a-versa. He would want you to sell when the market is already up. If you resist the sale, it would be a confirmation that the market is not only unrealistically up, but also overheated. Your reaction in great times is a clear signal of troubled times ahead (and vice versa). Your conviction that the market is headed to the next level, serves as an anti-data point for the great financial advisor. It will confirm that now is the best time to sell the holdings.

Anxiousness and excitement are related emotions in terms of your physical response. Both are emotions of arousal. When you are anxious or excited your heart beats faster, a hormone called cortisol spikes in your bloodstream and the body prepares for action. A great financial advisor will read these reactions as signs. If you are excited (which will typically happen at the top), he needs to be anxious and look forward to selling the holdings. On the other hand, if you are anxious (which typically happens at the bottom), he knows that it is time to buy and take full positions.

The good financial advisor and the great financial advisor probably get the same sort of returns. The difference is that the great financial advisor saves you a lot of volatility. The great financial advisor does this by sitting on cash for longer. This is called exposure. If a fund or a strategy has lesser exposure to the market but has the same returns as another one, which has more exposure, then the first one is a better option because it has better risk-adjusted returns (which is a metric to account for the degree of risk taken to achieve a certain return. Lesser risk for similar returns is always preferable). Better risk-adjusted returns imply that you do not react badly in times of trouble. This ensures that the investment journey is comfortable and doable.

Chapter 17

We are Designed to Ignore

The Comfort of Compound Interest

Sameer is not a qualified advisor on personal finance but he has a keen interest in the subject. He does think about money differently when it comes to his profession and his own finances. There are gaps there to be covered. However, amongst his friends, he is the finance guy and the investments expert. He is known to have the most organized personal finances and typically meets his goals on time. Having a reputation of being on target, he is often sought after by his friends to help them with their personal financial plans. One such couple is Dhriti and Aakash.

Dhriti and Akash are both MBAs. They have been together since the first year of the course. Dhriti is a product manager with a large e-tailer and Aakash manages the PnL for an entire product line of an FMCG company. Both work in Gurugram. Both are high earners. The household income is north of Rupees 6 million per annum. Even after paying EMIs for their apartment in World Spa and a shared large-sized executive sedan, their savings are still high. They have a collective saving valued north of Rupees 8 million.

Professionally, both Dhriti and Aakash are pressed for time. Dhriti ends up travelling 15 days a month at times and Aakash averages about 18 days a month. The house is practically run by the full-time house-keeper, who has been in service to Aakash since he was 9-years-old.

Financial planning is the buzz nowadays and Aakash and Dhriti too want to plan their finances. On a weekend, the couple invited Sameer over to their house, seeking help to sort out their financial plan.

Sameer took his laptop with his preloaded spreadsheets, ready to help his friends with their financial plan and the best-suited investment strategy. Having a broad idea about their financial goals, he was thinking about what their asset allocation should be, given their age and earning capacity. He would need to know each of their risk tolerances to make an optimal portfolio for them, individually and as a couple.

After having some coffee and inquiring about their current investments, Sameer got to know that Dhriti and Aakash's savings were completely deployed in fixed deposits. Fixed deposits or FDs, are the favourite instrument of Indians. Young or old, most of an Indian's financial life rotates around making and breaking the FD. If nothing needs to be done, the good folk at the bank simply roll over the FD for another period with the best interest rate that can be offered to the client. Of course, they do seek the approval of their esteemed clients.

Sameer was stunned after talking to the couple. Both Dhriti and Aakash were MBAs from a well-ranked business school. Yet, they had all their investments solely in FDs. After long and serious deliberation, he got to understand why they had invested all of the Rupees 8 million in FDs. The reasons were simple, clear, and precise.

The consolidated total figure of FD looked and felt great. The SMS alert showing the latest balance after a transaction was always a big morale booster. The total figure could be recalled anytime, through a single SMS, at an instant's notice. Rupees 8 million uniformly spread in chunks of 5 hundred thousand. Sixteen of those beautiful 500k babies. Each time Aakash thought about them, he could feel a warm tingle in his spine and almost a high. At the back of his mind, he knew something was wrong with this, but he always got swayed over.

Dhriti, on the other hand, felt the comfort and security of the figure. She had learnt that compound interest takes care of people in their later years. However, she too knew this may not be the optimal investment vehicle. That is why they had invited Sameer for helping them out and sorting things.

Thinking About the Present and the Future

Sameer had no reasonable explanation to give to himself on how this situation came to be. He explained to them that they needed to diversify even FDs, and expand their exposure to various asset classes. He explained to them about the two biggest inefficiencies and corpus destroyers of the personal finance cycle, which were inflation and taxes.

The post tax returns of their FDs should beat inflation or the very purpose of keeping money safe and accumulated may be defeated. Dhriti and Aakash would eventually end up losing the purchasing power of their savings. He also explained to them that even if they are risk-averse, they can tranche their investments in a way to only take a limited exposure, get much better returns, and beat inflation. For example, if they put some part of their money in a debt fund of government securities, they can save the tax component they were losing in FDs. This alone when compounded over many years would yield much more than FDs with lesser or the same amount of risk.

At the same time, Sameer explained to them that even if they do not need to get exposed to risk now, given that most of their targets are met or on track, it does not mean that they will not have new targets in the future. By allocating some component of their savings to equity, future goals like education of children (in case they plan to have them) could be funded much easily.

So they sat for another hour and discussed what the couple's plan should be to deploy the money over various assets and instruments over a period.

Sameer explained to them why they needed exposure to other forms of debt, gold, and equity for their financial assets to grow and give them worthy returns. Thereafter, Sameer parted with their friends, feeling satisfied on getting something right.

Three months later, out of friendly concern, Sameer followed up with the couple to see how they were progressing on the plan they had discussed. He was not surprised that they were still earning a 6% pre-tax interest rate on their savings. No action had been taken. This discussion did not produce a reaction, it was overcome by inertia.

Where Good Advice Gets Lost

It is not just the case with this professional couple, inaction is something that happens to all of us. When things are going good, we do not heed good advice, to make things better. We simply stay put. In fact, the only time we move to act is when we want to relieve some pain. In short, we only act upon "the urgent" (what we learnt in the last chapter) but not "the important," even if the evidence is clearly presented in front of us. In the case of Aakash and Dhriti, if they earn 6% in FDs which yields 4.5% post tax versus earning 7% in government bonds, the difference would be staggering. While INR 10 Million @7 % for 20 years amounts to INR 3,86,968,45/- at only 4.5% it yields INR 2,41,17140/-. This yields a difference of INR 1,457,971/-.

Heeding good advice to make things better, especially when times are good, is a tough thing to do. This inaction is called status quo bias. It means the current state of affairs of Aakash and Dhriti have become a baseline. Their minds have formed explanations around feeling high or secure respectively. Any change from this baseline is perceived as a loss. But why does this happen with our finances, even though we know the importance of money? There are plenty of reasons which we can understand by delving into the psyche of Aakash and Dhriti.

Firstly, when the real decision, whether to expose their savings to the market or not, comes, the couple may suddenly become loss-averse. This means that they weigh potential losses more than the potential gains. Even though they know that long-term participation in the stock markets will help them gain much more than the FDs, the negative news and stories weigh heavier. The anticipated regret of loss hurts more than the potential gains. This phenomenon is called loss-aversion. Loss-aversion is not logical, yet the behaviour is prevalent.

We do not discuss things with others about situations we are comfortable about (we only discuss pain). Therefore, we do not know that there can be better alternatives to our current state of comfort. It is not that people don't like taking risks. What people don't like is losing things. We feel losses twice as keenly as we feel gains. So, we hate losing Rs 100 as much as we like making Rs 200.

Next, the couple continues to invest in the same type of instrument i.e. FDs. This is because the more they have invested in an option, the more are they likely to continue with it. They do not want to contradict their previous decisions. They feel that over time the current option will turn out to be the best option. This behaviour is called sunk cost fallacy. By being invested in FDs, their returns are not just physical, but psychological as well. The human perspective triumphs over the financial perspective. The cost of change is high, especially because it involves calling their past selves wrong. It simply hurts to admit that you were wrong and mend your ways. Instead, it is easier to cover it up and keep moving in the same direction, all because the mind justifies it with a single statement that *"if it ain't broke, don't fix it."*

Thirdly, when the couple received a suggestion which did not match their current pattern of thinking, they felt a cognitive dissonance. This means they have competing urges, involving conflicting attitudes, beliefs, or behaviour. For example, when you want to eat a slice of chocolate mud cake, you know the amount of sugar in the cake slice is harmful for you (cognition). Yet, another part of you wants to wipe it clean (behaviour). This is a state of cognitive dissonance.

On one hand, Aakash and Dhriti want to improve their investing outcomes because at an intellectual level they know that the current investment patterns might make them fall short of their long term desires. On the other hand, they feel the high and comfort of the figure and its consistency in the present time. These competing urges or future thought versus present experience cause a decision paralysis. They want to act, but cannot act. This leaves their finances in limbo.

Finally, the high earning, highly educated couple tends to stay with the familiar. The mere exposure to the FDs as an investment instrument makes it a comfortable option. They know how FDs and the process around them works. It is familiar. We may argue that in the digital age it is as easy to open an investing account as it is to renew an FD. However, after that step, things become new and unfamiliar. As a default, the couple does not want to take the effort to learn more about something new. Perhaps they are pressed by time and commitments. Perhaps it is just difficult. Perhaps they don't want to move out of the comfort zone. FDs are easy for them.

The "Talk About It" Strategy

There is plenty of good advice out there. It seldom changes. However, our design prevents us from taking action. Sameer understands that changing behaviour requires changes in habits. Setting simple rules helps too. Changing habits work much like compounding. Small gradual improvements over time pay off in big ways. A focus on process is what produces gradual improvement.

Though discouraged by the behaviour of Aakash & Dhriti, Sameer takes heart from this Agatha Christie quote:

> *"Good advice is always certain to be ignored,*
> *but that's no reason not to give it."*

So, we have a simple, yet effective strategy for you to overcome inaction. We simply call it the "talk -about -it" strategy.

In this strategy, you first acknowledge that there are some investing habits you need to change. It would be great if you know exactly what to change. However, it is okay if you do not. Next, talk about it. Remember to only talk, not act on what you get through conversations.

Typically, 2-3 professional experts are required to gain good know-how. Pitch your problem area to these people. Record the responses on how they approach the problem and what solution they would follow. The entire process may take a couple of months (considering you will not be doing this full-time). Also, be careful that you may be getting response as per their own biases and that may need to be discounted.

We suggest you do not talk to other investors because their goals and needs may be much different from yours. You may still need growth, whereas they might have already achieved their goals. Therefore, your strategy requirements will be much different than theirs. This will colour your view unnecessarily.

After you are comfortable with this new knowledge, hire a professional to help you with a plan and execute it.

Chapter 18

How We Make Tough Decisions

The Exporter's Ventures

Rahul's wool garments export business began in December of 2002. Initially, he sourced the garments from manufacturers in Ludhiana, labelled them, and shipped them in containers to fulfil orders placed by large retail chains in the US and Europe. The setup worked amazingly. He would often make 200% profit on most shipments. However, the reliability of these shipments was not under his control. Rahul was dependent on his suppliers. He thought to himself, 'If I am procuring the finished goods at X price, then it must be that the manufacturer would be making profits as well.' If he could manufacture the goods himself then it would mean his profits would increase substantially and it shall also give him control over his supplies. So, with the insistence and support of his large clients, he set up his first manufacturing unit in 2005.

By then, his investments in the stock markets had already paid-off well and he was pumping more money into the markets. The good investing results gave him comfort and the confidence spilt into taking more and more calculated risks in the wool garments business. By 2007, he was managing 3 units, 2 of which he had started on his own in Gurugram and Ludhiana, and a third which he had taken over, which was located in Ludhiana as well.

Business boomed and profits poured in. However, in 2008, the stock markets crashed and Rahul's stock portfolio lost a good part of its value. Once again, with Mr Prakash's counsel, he stayed invested in the markets and much of the value recovered by the end of 2009. By now, Rahul had already purchased 3 commercial properties and the rentals were good enough to cover his life's expenses. So Rahul was truly free to take risks and grow his wealth.

Rahul was buying and selling in properties as well but limited his exposure to 1 to 2 deals at a time. He understood real estate as an asset class quite well. Some of the properties he had bought in 2011 got held up because the market was slow. He was only able to sell in 2016 at a nominal profit. However, this did not matter because his other investments were paying off well and his business was booming. He was manufacturing and marketing his own apparel brand and was profitable in each one of his now seven units of garment production.

In late 2016, Rahul got an offer from one of his customers, a large international fashion house, to buy his businesses altogether. He was offered 10 times the value of sales of his business. It was an offer Rahul could not refuse. He thought to himself that it was time he retired from the garments line. He now wanted to try his hand at other things. The deal went through in mid of 2017 and Rahul had already made plans to deploy the money. His new area of focus was going to be Angel Investing. All around his friends had put money into venture funds and were sitting on huge valuations of the startups the funds had invested in. Rahul decided he wanted in, and in a big way.

Rahul had been studying SaaS (Software as a Service) start-ups for a while now. He was very clear that the investments in tech-based startups would really pay off. The trick was to get in early. Over a period of 3 months, Rahul had studied 3 angel-funded startups. He liked the founders and believed in their models. So within a span of 2 months, he deployed 25% of his funds into the three companies and became an early-stage investor. Rahul was confident that with his business experience in the wool garments industry, he would be able to steer the 3 teams in a good direction. He envisaged that within 2 years he would be able to help them scale up and make huge returns on exits.

In 2019, the 3 investments, worth 25% of his business proceeds, were still struggling to turn profit. 2 of the 3 companies desperately needed more cash just to keep operations afloat and pay salaries. The third was ready to go deep into the red within a few months. Rahul had tried to get more investors to pool in funds so the businesses could perhaps stay afloat. However, everyone told him that he himself should put in more money instead. Unwilling to risk more capital, he was stuck. The unicorn potential startups were haemorrhaging cash and now looked like no good duds.

Life is Unfair

Rahul has been lucky in his stock market investing, real estate investments, and garments business, yet life has been unfair to him at least 2 times.

In the first instance, Rahul got to make a major investment decision very early on in life. He had little information about what he was getting into. He had no prior experience either in stock markets or in the wool garments business. Either of them could have turned sour. In each case, Rahul would have lost money and suffered bitterly. His lessons would have been very different and the path of his life would have been much ordinary. It was only luck that he had a good advisor like Mr Prakash or that he was a part of the garments industry and property boom in the early stages. However, the choice he was offered was unfair because he did not have complete information to make that decision. He did not know what would work out or not.

In the second case, Rahul's success got the better of him. His success in the garment business gave him confidence. This confidence made him feel sure of his abilities to manage a new business. It made him foray into new areas he had no expertise in. Subsequently, he overlooked key signs of success and failure in the ventures he invested in. Failure generally comes from a failure to imagine negative eventualities, and not being able to prepare for them. Rahul could have never predicted the outcome of these investments because of their nature. Yet he decided to go ahead.

Finally, when these investments came to a juncture where more money was required to be pumped in, he could not decide. He lost his confidence and the decision became tough.

Life is unfair to all of us. We get to make all the important decisions early on. What type of education to pursue, which profession to choose, whom to marry, etc. These are important, yet tough decisions which have long-term repercussions. Moreover, we have no experience (or enough data) to make these decisions in our teen years or in our twenties, or even our thirties. There is simply no way of knowing how these decisions will turn out because of external factors.

You cannot simply know whether doing an engineering degree today will be useful 10 years later. You cannot know your spouse will support you or drag you down 5 years later. Or even moving to a new country with promising options may turn out well or change into a bad choice. Each of these scenarios has two problems that make it a tough decision.

1. You are *unable to see the larger picture* because either the known options are not clear-cut (or fuzzy), or the alternatives to these options are unknown to you.
2. We are *unable to envisage the long-term outcome* of the decisions we make now because there are too many variables that can happen between now and then.

In short,

$$(Fuzzy/\ Unknown\ Options) * (Fuzzy/\ Unknown\ Outcomes) = Tough\ Decision$$

How We Make Tough Decisions

When faced with uncertainty, the human perspective kicks in. Instead of doing deep research, we tend to rely on advice from others. In some cases, parents help, at other times, teachers or even friends show the way. In Rahul's case, he had Mr Prakash's guidance. Taking help is the default strategy available to anyone who wants to make tough decisions. At other times, we do follow our hearts. Sometimes it works, sometimes it does not.

The tough decision problems extend to personal finance as well. When making financial decisions, we do not see the entire picture. The options available are not clear-cut and neither do we know all the possible alternatives for investing our money. Even more, we do not know how these decisions will turn out. So what do we do?

Well, to our observation, most of the people do two things.

Overextending Your Expertise

If you are already successful in your careers, either making good money, commanding a high position, or even topping your class, you are likely to carry the monetary success, executive ability, or academic performance into your investing. This is going to give you confidence and you are likely to make decisions on the same lines as your career or education. Confidence in one area can cause overconfidence in another.

We are likely to overestimate our ability in making decisions mostly because we might have a track-record in one aspect of business or profession or education. This is not because we are casual about it, but because our brain works on models. Once we experience a successful model, we are likely to unknowingly extend its functionality to other areas. However, not all models work everywhere. Realizing this later in life costs dearly.

We have known numerous examples where retired service officials have lost their entire gratuity in 3 months, trading options on a single stock. Ph. D. students have lost their tuition fees numerous times by investing through a model they were researching on. Even successful executives have invested and lost their entire net worth in a single startup. Extending our expertise is in our nature.

Most of the people will not acknowledge that their job or business is only a part of their financial portfolio. It is the only part of their portfolio, in which they are an expert. However, what takes up most of your time becomes the most important thing in your life. Reassigning its status as "part of your portfolio" is difficult. Yet, from the financial perspective, your job or business is only part of your financial portfolio. It is the only part you are an expert at. Chances are this expertise may not be good knowledge in other areas.

Relying on Others' Overextended Expertise

On the contrary, if you do not carry the baton of success and confidence, then you will turn for advice to the same well-wishers as before - parents, friends, and relatives. This is because you trust them. They have helped you before. Here too you are likely to extend "the extent of their wisdom" from one area to another. This tendency is called the halo effect.

The well-wishing advisor will gladly help you out of the goodness of their hearts. Their confidence will perhaps come from their success in any other field. However, the fact that the well-wisher may only be as average as you in the area of finances is invariably overlooked. Typically, people are not experts in more than one or two areas. Yet, when giving advice, they extend their expertise into areas they have no experience in. This is due to the outcome bias, wherein we judge and evaluate past decisions on the quality of the outcome rather than the quality of a decision.

In other cases, you may be impressed by the success story of your friend. The one silver-bullet investment he made and made a fortune out of it. It is the one investment that fixed all his worries for life. Hearing the story, you are likely to be motivated and act in the same way. Your brain makes a story by stitching random happenings into a perfectly logical chain of events. It starts to believe that there is a cause-effect relationship and that you can explain things. While it may have worked well for your friend, it may not work out well for you because the conditions around the investment might have changed or perhaps he was just lucky. Acting upon narratives of success often leads to poor outcomes in investing. The story counts, but no one looks into the reasons for success. It pays to remember that you are susceptible to the narrative fallacy as well.

Apart from these pitfalls, a lot more biases, fallacies and effects come into play in our investment decision-making process. Some of the common ones are:

- Analysis paralysis (where you analyze to the point you cannot make a decision)
- Recency effect (where you give more weight to present information than earlier information)
- Herd mentality (where you intend to find comfort and justification of your action because everyone else is doing it)
- Urgency effect (where you hear something sensational and feel the urge to do something)

The list of pitfalls is long. Then how do we make investing decisions with a good probability of success? Hope is not lost.

Less is More

The first step to avoid the biases in investing is to acknowledge that they exist. This will help you rephrase the question,

"Should I invest in this opportunity?"

to

"What do I know about this opportunity?"

The likely answer will be "not much." If you feel compelled to seek others' advice, extend the question to them as well,

"What does the person I am intending to seek advice from, know about this investment?"

If the answer again is "not much," bypass them too.

A lot of people have a great need to understand the workings of an investment. They need exact answers and precise understanding of the underlying mechanisms of an investment. If they find a compelling logic to an investment, they are sold on to it. Such logic is often based on compelling narratives. People who have a greater need to understand everything, are often the most vulnerable and easily fall for the narratives. So they need to shut narratives out to think clearly. In order to do this, they need to turn off the TV, not research the internet or newspapers, and be sceptical of writings which are painted narratives but claim to be facts. The lesser they know, the more likely they are not going to reverberate the existing facts. This will help them avoid confirmation bias.

Finally, apply the crossed-box framework to check the authenticity of an investment. If it holds the relationships in the test, it is likely a good investment. Dip a toe and gain experience before you jump in.

Systematic Investing

An even better strategy to make tough investment decisions is to not let yourself come to the point where you have to make that decision. This can be done by fully committing to systematic investing. A good investing system will allocate 100% of your available funds and not leave you with any room to get tempted. Here, 100% allocation does not mean you are 100% invested all the time. A good investment system will allocate funds to cash as well. 100% allocation means that there are no idle funds lying to play with. All funds have a purpose. This means you do not get to exercise your choices, and neither do you get played by your biases or others' biases. A good system will need good implementation as well. This can be done with the help of a financial advisor. Thoughtfully designed and rigorously followed systems win, always.

Chapter 19

─── ◆ ───

Hopes and Dreams

Dreams of B-Schoolers

Let us share with you a real-life happening. In 2018, we were invited by the students of a top-ranked business school to conduct a small workshop on personal finance. The class was going to graduate in a few months. About 95% of the class was already placed in the best companies with high paying jobs. Some of the students were already up with plans for entrepreneurship and were in the process of getting funding as well. The students wanted a heads up on the topic of personal finance since they would now be making good amounts of money and wanted to put it to good use.

The format of the workshop was interactive. We presented the students with some models on how they could do well with their personal finances in the future. We also talked about the topics which form the content of this book - markets, finance, and perspectives around finance. Some of the ideas and strategies we shared resonated well with them and some topics were bounced by them, while a few ideas were outrightly rejected. (It is a smart strategy not to argue with the coming generation's top talent, especially if they disagree with your views!).

The human aspect of finance always gets in the way of learning, but we understand that it is a long-term process to hone the financial perspective. The workshop lasted about 2 hours. We were happy to have suggested some good ideas to the students and by them picking up those ideas.

After the workshop, the students wanted a Q&A session. Most questions were a validation of their future plans. The first thing everyone wanted to do was to pay off their education loans. They planned to do this within the next 3 years instead of 7. We vehemently agreed with this, since the only time you should not pay off a personal financial liability sooner is when you can earn a sure-shot 5% over the interest rate you are paying. This means if you borrowed the money at 10% interest rate, then only if you make 15% should you keep paying the EMI instead of down-paying the loan faster. We were happy with this. Perhaps it was the workshop's learning or perhaps just good values.

We expected that the next aspiration for business school graduates would be to invest in stock markets and build themselves a portfolio. After all, with the kind of salaries these students would be getting, it would easily put them in the top 1% of the salaried income earners in India. They could spend well, but still save enough to invest well. On top of it, these students grew up in the era when investing was in vogue and they had only recently studied finance and business.

However, we were surprised that investing in stock markets did not rank number 2 on the list. The second aspiration (after paying off their loans) for most of the students was buying a house. While this was okay for someone who did not have their own house as yet, it was not the case with most students.

We learnt that even when some students already had a family home which they were expecting to inherit, they still wanted a new house either to upgrade the existing one or for "investment purposes". Others were only 25 and were ready to invest in a house already. This intrigued us.

Real estate as an asset class was high on the investment list. We had explained the CAGR concept and how stocks could still be a better option.

Yet, the human perspective was still overshadowing the financial perspective, even after a top-notch MBA training.

Your House is an Asset, But Not Always…

There are a lot of theories which tell you when it is optimal to buy a house. Some indicate the right age is 35, some 40, and some suggest even later in life. Other theories talk about income levels or savings levels and priorities of personal needs. But nowhere is it suggested that you should aim to buy a house at the age of 27 (the average age of the students in the session). We explained to the students that buying a house at 27 years of age was not a very wise move.

We even explained the math around it and showed how they would be better off investing in higher-paying assets like equity (compounding is better when you start early). We even argued that a house is a long-term commitment. They may not even be living in the same city in a few years. The logical arguments bounced and the aspiration to buy a house stood strong. So we decided to inquire further. The first layer of arguments for buying a second house or at a younger age sounded like:

"Why pay rent when you can pay an EMI?"

"It is a long term investment that eventually goes up!"

"Be sorted with it (permanent accommodation) now, rather than later."

"You can lease it, if you don't use it."

We had heard these marketed *fundas* before. The programming is done through propaganda by builders and bankers. It sounds so easy on the television commercial. "Apna Ghar" resonates comfortably with our most basic desire for shelter. Yet everything that is marketed to us, is already sold to us by ourselves. The marketing is just a reinforcement.

Mom Said So...

We decided to dig a bit more. We asked why buying a house was important and on whose advice were they acting? The question hit the spot. The answer in each case was nearly identical:

> *"Because my mother told me so."*
> *"It is my mother's dream to have our own townhouse."*
> *"My mom always wanted us to live in a 4 bedroom..."*

Mom. Mother. Mama. Our life's first love. Our first caregiver. Our first friend and confidant. Our first teacher, and also the first person to discipline us. If a request comes from our mother, we are not likely to refuse it (much to the disappointment of our spouses as well!). We never question an emotional request made by our mothers. We consider it as an order. In fact, we make it our mission, without any questions asked.

The Successful Life Plan

Parents in India are programmed to incessantly pursue their children to follow 'The Successful Life Plan'. They want us to get good grades, pursue good degrees, work in a great job, get a prestigious car, get happily married, buy a dream house, and have loving children. Then, as grandparents, the second innings begins. They then push us, their children, to do the same for their grandchildren. The whole cycle is well oiled and highly functional. It has been going on for generations.

Buying a house is a part of this plan, so is getting a great job and a prestigious car. In fact, entire advertising campaigns are built on this success plan. Any business which understands the plan and has a product or service that can be a part of the plan, uses it to sell their goods. A car becomes a "family car". An apartment becomes a "dream home" or "apna ghar" and so on. Parents, spouses, and children or anyone who has an emotional influence over us, are also influenced by these agendas. These agendas eventually seep into our personal finance decisions as well.

There is nothing wrong in following the successful life plan. It is good advice for a good life, except that perhaps it carries the agenda of a different generation. These agendas are called inherited biases. They always come in the guise of hopes and dreams. Hopes and dreams that have been learnt. Hopes and dreams that are perhaps not our own. Hopes and dreams that no one questions.

The agenda becomes a self-sustaining cycle. The children do not want to question the parent's wish because they may feel it is disrespectful to disagree. So they follow the agenda. The parents do not suggest the children do anything otherwise, lest that option does not work out. So everyone agrees to the standard-one-size-fits-all format of life. This is called Abilene paradox. Abilene paradox is a form of groupthink. It was described in the book *The Abilene Paradox and Other Meditations on Management* by Jerry B. Harvey.

The Abilene paradox describes a situation in a family of four. The family is bored and wants to do something. The father suggests going for dinner to Abilene which is a one-hour drive from their home. None of the family members really wants to go there. However, everyone thinks that everyone else wants to go there, but is afraid to speak up as well. This often happens to us in person with our financial decisions. Parents think that children want a standard-one-size-fits-all life. They want to keep their advice within the safe limits of the successful life plan. Children, on the other hand, think that the parents' advice is their hopes and dreams. They feel obligated to fulfil them. Consequently, a lot of unwanted financial inventory gets accumulated.

The parents, who expect their children to follow the successful life plan, unknowingly push their children to make long and deep financial commitments. They overlook the fact that presently a car is becoming redundant because ride-hailing services are more practical (or at least they were pre-COVID, and still may be once we start living with it), work is moving to home, or that you may be travelling for the most part of a month. A house can be not useful if your line of work requires you to move to a different city every three years. Following the prevalent agenda is a behavioural gap that we learn. The parents are not wrong, but you can disagree.

Surprisingly, they may agree to your disagreement with the agenda. From there on, you can all make better purchase and investment decisions as a family. Breaking group-think only requires asking the preference of the individuals of the group and voicing your opinion in a group forum. It gets down to separating emotional preferences from life's requirements and working towards them as per your capacity.

Wants, Affordability, and Needs

How you take up investment risk is very closely related to these three things - your wants, needs, and affordability. Let us take a look at the three.

Wants are all about feelings. We want bigger, better, and more expensive things. However, we want to have them in the least risky way. We may want to earn 12% returns on our investments. However, we may also not want to put our hard-earned money in equity and choose to put them in safe and secured fixed deposits. The problem is that fixed deposits do not earn 12% returns. At the time of writing this book, they earn around 5%. Wants emanate from how we feel about things. Many times these things are out of sync with reality and are unreasonable.

Separate from feelings and much more connected to reality is affordability. Affordability is related to how much money is available to us for spending or taking up risks. Affordability is mathematical and ends up directing our decision making. For example, we can only afford a house which falls into our budget or only make investments which are within the range of our ticket size. Affordability is realistic. If we do something we cannot afford, then reality puts us into our place sooner or later.

Finally, there are needs. Needs too are real in the present. This means if you are a family of two today, you really do not need a house bigger than 2 bedrooms at present. However, needs change with time. This means you may need a bigger house later if you are planning to grow your family. When assessing our needs, we need to be a bit forward-thinking and factor in the future as well, especially for larger spends.

Similar to affordability, needs too are real and quantifiable. If what you need is less than what you can afford, then you will be satisfied and vice versa. This satisfaction is the financial perspective. Affordability dictates our needs. Simply put,

$$Satisfaction = f(Affordability > Need)$$

Yet the factor of wants distorts our thinking. You may need a three-bedroom house taking into consideration the future. This house will come in various forms and localities at various costs. Some of these costs you may easily be able to afford. Some might be stretched for you. Here, your wants come into play and affect your decision-making. There is always a house you may like a lot but cannot afford practically. There is always a negotiation between your wants and affordability, and that represents the human perspective. If what you want costs less than what you can afford, then you will be happy. Simply put:

$$Happiness = f(Affordability > Want)$$

The Three Finger Rule - Being Happy and Satisfied

The negotiable relation between wants and affordability and the dictatorship relation between needs and affordability can be easily mastered using the three finger rule. By understanding this rule not only can you make better financial decisions, but also stay happy.

Take the three fingers of your hand - the index finger, the middle finger, and the ring finger. Typically, for most people, the middle finger is the tallest, the ring finger is of middle height, and the index finger is the shortest. Now quantify the value of your wants, your affordability, and your needs. In order to see whether you will be satisfied and happy at the end of a financial decision, simply assign the highest value to your middle finger, the least value to your index finger, and the middle value to your ring finger. Table 10 will show you the outcome of your decision.

Table 10: The Three Finger Rule

Middle Finger (Tallest)	Ring Finger (Middle)	Index Finger (Shortest)	Human Perspective (Affordability > Want)	Financial Perspective (Affordability > Need)	State
Want	Need	Afford	Unhappy	Unsatisfied	Misery
Want	Afford	Need	Unhappy	Satisfied	Greed
Afford	Need	Want	Happy	Satisfied	Contentment
Afford	Want	Need	Happy	Satisfied	Aspirational
Need	Afford	Want	Happy	Unsatisfied	Denial
Need	Want	Afford	Unhappy	Unsatisfied	Despair

Chapter 20

In For The Long Term

The BTST Investor

Sanjoy Sen, Sameer's boss, is a well experienced corporate man and wise with his wealth. However, wisdom always comes at a cost. The least cost paid for getting wise is by making mistakes and learning from them, called experience.

In 2007, whilst still in his 30s, Sanjoy was very active in stock markets. The market was great for jobbers (people who scalp the markets by buying huge numbers of lots in the future markets and then selling them the very next instant at 2-5 ticks). Jobbers were full-time traders, engaged in the market from 9 am to 3:30 pm. The second best thing to do, especially if you were not a full-time trader, was to work with BTST calls. BTST refers to buying today at the closing price and selling tomorrow at open. In a bull market, when all stocks are moving up, this technique works very well. It uses momentum as an underlying anomaly and gives wonderful results. BTST was also referred to as "buying the candle".

A bull market brings a set of specialized services offered by research houses. Most experts who appear on TV also provide services which offer research calls to act upon. Sanjoy too subscribed for such a stock tip service. The trial period was for 2 weeks with research calls being given for stocks to be bought or sold within 1 to 5 days. Sanjoy took the trial period for a week. During this time, he followed the service religiously using the entry prices, stop-loss, and exit targets. The service was genuinely good. Sanjoy made good profits following its calls.

By the end of the week, Sanjoy realized he had already earned the amount that the service was asking for a 6 months period. Seeing it as a no-loss venture, Sanjoy subscribed to the advance package of the service for a period of 6 months. A month later, the market boomed and Sanjoy made supernormal profits using the service. He now had a cushion of profits to work with.

On the next buying call that the service gave, Sanjoy decided to experiment a bit. He thought to himself that it would be just during this one call that he would break the discipline. He already had a cushion of profits to bank upon. After all, how would he learn and develop his own method of analysis if he did not experiment, he felt. He was an MBA from a top business school. He just had to have his own method!

So, Sanjoy bought the day's call but did not sell the stock at the target price prescribed. He held on and kept the stock a bit longer. The day after, the market moved up even further and the stock led the way! A week later, Sanjoy was sitting on double the amount of profit he would have made if he had sold the stock at the prescribed exit price. Sanjoy realized that he had a hunch on the stock because he had done a bit of research on its fundamentals. The price-to-earnings ratio was low and the sales growth was high over the past year. He concluded that this is a good way to screen and select good stocks.

The data about these ratios were available through reports on the internet. After 3 weeks, he had a bunch of stocks in his portfolio. The returns were better than the stock tip service's targets, plus he thought to himself that if he held these gems for over a year, these investments would qualify for long term capital gains as well. He would pay no taxes and could keep all the profits. He concluded that the stock-tip service was a good starting point, but his own method on top of that was better than that.

A few months later, the earnings for the stocks Sanjoy owned came soft. The market corrected a bit. Sanjoy felt this was only temporary and the markets would recover soon. After another 3 months, the market had not recovered. There was talk of a global crisis and recession. Half of the good stocks he owned were down by 25% and the other half had recovered a bit to the initial levels. Sanjoy decided that if he sold some of the winners, he would cover up for the losses of these gems. He thought to himself, if the market goes up he would recover everything with the stocks moving back to previous highs.

Another 3 months down the news said that the economy was in a full-blown recession. Sanjoy's portfolio of gems was down by 50%. He thought to himself that he could not get out now. Two of the companies in his portfolio suddenly declared bankruptcy. These companies cited unserviceable debt and promoter issues. The rest of the companies were distressed too. Sanjoy could probably have sold and recovered at least 50% of his investment. However, he decided that it is better to be in the market for the long term.

Long Term Investment

"It is a long term investment."

We have heard these words innumerable times as a simple and easy justification for any investment action gone bad. In fact, we are so tuned to the adage, that as soon as we hear it, we jump on our feet, with our eyes and ears open, and a bit of pulse racing. Why? Because most of the long-term investments did not start with the same intention.

Long-term portfolios consisting of really bad stocks are very common. We have known several investors who have portfolios full of infrastructure and construction companies at $1/10^{th}$ of their value from 2007. Research shows that 95% of these stocks will never recover even to their original purchase value. Yet, the investors do not sell these stocks to even recover the 10%, because they feel they need to be made whole from the unjustified loss they have suffered. They justify these unresolved feelings by telling themselves that it is a long-term investment.

This is the human perspective of investing. It directly contradicts the financial perspective of investing. While it is for the long term betterment of the investors to get rid of these holdings, they seldom do. Not selling a stock which has fallen by 90% is called loss-aversion.

Investors hate losses almost two times as much as they love gains. This phenomenon is explained by 'prospect theory' which was formulated in 1979 by Amos Tversky and Nobel Laureate Daniel Kahneman and was further developed upon in later years. Loss-aversion is such a strong behaviour in investing that it makes investors risk-seeking in hopes that they will recover their investment somehow. Many long term portfolios are actually a result of loss-aversion. Investors want to cover their losses and in the process seek even more risks, accumulating duds after duds.

The process starts with the thought, 'How much more can I lose,' or 'How much more can it go down further?' This is the common refrain of an investor when a stock has fallen more than 75% and let's say the price comes down to Rs 10 from Rs 40, not realising that if it falls further down to Rs 5, it will still be a 50% fall from Rs 10, resulting in a further 50% loss. The same Rs 10 invested elsewhere would possibly have a better chance of recovery than this stock due to better fundamentals or valuations.

Deep losses in one set of stocks at a particular time are rarely recovered by the same set of stocks. They are almost always recovered by a different set of stocks or perhaps maybe a different type of investment altogether. The same happens with real estate investments that did not move back up or other types of assets like cryptocurrencies. Investors who bought it at the top, wait for the top.

An Emotional Affair

We are designed to stick to a brand name. That is why branding is such a successful strategy. Once we spend time with something, the emotional cost of switching is difficult to overcome. This switching cost is even higher if the emotions behind it are of the extreme sort. In investing this means that if you made a huge profit or a huge loss from an instrument, you are likely going to stick to it in the future for emotional reasons.

In Sanjoy's case, he did not come to lose 50% of the portfolio value over 1 single day or even a month. It was over a period of time with multiple decisions in the same direction. Is it Sanjoy's fault? Not really. He, like the rest of us, is hardwired to make certain errors, over and over again. The first hardwired error was overconfidence. Sanjoy overestimated his ability to predict the stock market's future. He experimented with some of his own actions and was successful. His brain took this success as a feedback and came to a conclusion. Then this conclusion made him overconfident and thus less cautious. The overconfidence let him deviate from the plan. One of the reasons for deviation was the lack of human oversight to ensure he stuck to it. Had Sanjoy been consulting a human advisor, rather than an internet-based service, he could have been talked out of his analysis system.

The next hardwired error is the disposition effect. It is our tendency to sell assets which have increased in value and keep assets which have fallen in value. This is why Sanjoy decided to keep the losers and sell winners to make up for the losses of the losers. Disposition effect is a very common behaviour in investing. It occurs because we significantly dislike losing in comparison to winning.

Surprisingly, even though the tax law discourages the disposition effect by rewarding investors for long-term investments and taxing them for short-term gains. Yet investors end up with long term losses and much lower short-term gains. In an ideal world, Sanjoy would keep the winners and cut short the losers. This would amount to long term gains and short term losses (which, from a tax point of view, is a better scenario to be in).

Long-term investment ends being used as a term for investments where the investor does not know how to get out, and does not want to acknowledge the loss because of the pain associated with it and is stuck with them. In some cases, investors commit even more funds by averaging on the way down. Averaging on a bad stock is an escalation of commitment. At the time of writing this book, we know of a lot of investors who are averaging in a certain banking stock for almost the past 2 years. They simply want to recover their money from that stock only. The stock ended up being put on a selling moratorium for 2 years by the regulator. Instead of looking elsewhere, the investors are only averaging the stock. Averaging is an advanced tool for the tactical fund manager. It is not to be used by investors. In the long term, investors only end up having an emotional affair with such stocks.

How to Long Term Invest?

The simple answer is through managed portfolios or indices. Portfolios are essentially a bunch of investments. They consist of many instruments instead of just one or a few. Further, they are managed by some principles of money management and strategies to generate returns with a limited or known amount of risk.

In stocks, the simplest portfolio is an index. You can invest in the index using an index fund or ETFs. The index is a known formula. It has a known composition and is essentially diversified (broadly or within a particular sector). Alternately, you can invest through broadly diversified mutual funds. So, what about the behaviours that get us stuck with dud stocks? Can those be mitigated using an index based or managed portfolio? Let us answer these questions:

1. Should you average in an index when the market falls? YES, you can. A market capitalization based index always recovers. The Sensex has its volatility and has maintained its upward trajectory and shall continue to do so till the economy is growing or the investors feel that it has the potential to grow. Overtime losing companies are replaced by winning companies. (The same may not be true for sectoral or thematic indices. We suggest you do not average those indices).

2. Should you sell a winning Index and buy more of the lesser performing one? YES, you can. An expensive market is likely to come down or underperform in the coming months in comparison to an inexpensive market (unless there is something structurally wrong with the

inexpensive market). This is called regression to the mean. It happens over long periods of time.

3. Can you time the market or have confidence in your ability to figure tops and bottoms? YES and NO. You cannot time the exact top or bottom - never! In general, tops are harder to predict than bottoms. The stock market doesn't go minus, so if you buy after a crash or correction, you are likely to make good money out of it because there is a margin of safety. Have confidence in your ability to buy cheap. (This also may not hold true of a stock. It may hold true of an index or a mutual fund. Stocks can almost hit zero, delist, or become non-tradeable).

4. Will you be marred by switching cost on an index? Not really. There are not many options for a capitalization based index. You can buy the NIFTY or the SENSEX, it is practically the same from a returns perspective.

Further, professionally managed portfolios like mutual funds or equity advised portfolios for average investors, and portfolio management systems (PMS) or alternate investment funds (AIF) for high net worth investors are also a good way to invest for the long term. You only have to manage yourself in one way to do this. Stick to the option for the long term. The active manager ensures that your investment value stays up by losing the bad stocks from time to time and stacking up on the winners.

Note: Using Disposition Effect to Our Advantage

It is worth mentioning here that the disposition effect can be used to our advantage as well, albeit some conditions are in place. It is a fallacy to think that stocks will mean revert i.e., winners will fall and losers will rise in time frames such as 6 months to 2 years. However, over longer periods of time, asset classes and portfolios do tend to revert to mean.

NY Stern School of Business's finance professor Aswath Damodaran found that,

> *"Future 10-year stock market return premiums are negatively correlated to historical stock market premiums."*

This translates to the fact that if stock markets have performed well as an asset class in recent years, then they may perform poorly in the coming years. Equity or stock market returns like other assets are cyclical. Mean reversion is a well-observed phenomenon in asset classes (with some accuracy) such as gold, fixed income, and equities. These asset classes rise and fall more than they are expected to and then come back to their original path. However, profiting from this mean reversion is a matter of timing, something at which humans consistently perform poorly.

Mean reversion also takes place in stock portfolios such as mutual funds. In their 2016 research paper titled "*The Harm in Selecting Funds that Have Recently Outperformed*", the three researchers Bradford Cornell, Jason Hsu, and David Nanigian point out that,

> *"Based on portfolios constructed using U.S. mutual fund data over typical three-year evaluation periods, we find that investors who chose funds with poor recent performance earned higher excess returns than those who chose funds with superior recent performance."*

This means that if you buy equity mutual funds based on their recent performance, you will underperform the markets. A contrarian strategy may work. It is important to remember that mutual funds are diversified portfolios based on the investing style of the manager or a strategy. We do not suggest you follow this approach yourself. It is best to consult an investment professional for the same.

Chapter 21

The DIY Gap

The DSLR Camera

On Myra's first birthday, Priya and Sameer had organized a party. The guest list grew to 150, so they decided to book a banquet hall in a hotel. Priya is fond of good decoration and chose a light pink decor with matching balloons and stars. Next, the menu was set by Priya's mom. She is a Delhi socialite who knew what exactly needed to be on the menu. Alongside, a kids games package was also included. Finally, Priya's dad suggested that the whole event needed to be photographed and videos were to be made as well. So an elite team of photographers was called upon. The team was expensive. While Sameer was okay to foot the bill for the venue, the food, the decoration, and everything else, the photographer's bill hurt him. He was not able to justify to himself why a team of 3 people needed to be paid Rupees 60,000 for only 4 hours of coverage. Sure the pictures came out good, but Sameer and Priya had to wait for 3 months for the album and another month for the video. The joy of reliving the sweet emotional moments was delayed. In Sameer's heart, it was not a delay, but denial. According to him, he had already paid an unjustified amount, and then everyone had been kept on hold for an unjustified time as well.

What is there in a camera, Sameer thought. It's just a few clicks and everything is digital. Softwares are easily available to correct the lighting, colours, and other technicalities. So he thought to himself that he should not be paying for such a thing. Photography is much easier than finance. If he can understand and tweak parameters to manage the risk of a portfolio, why should photography be difficult! So began his research into photography. The first few websites he opened told him it was all about just three things - aperture, shutter speed, and ISO. Sameer delved into the technical details of the 3 pillars of photography.

Next, he learnt that white balance also played a vital role in getting the colours right in the first go. So he mastered the concept of colour temperature as well. He concluded that a good camera is one which allows you to easily manage these options on the go. Further, it provides you with dedicated buttons for these functions as well as the bracketing function to click those HDR photos. An advanced device allows multi-point focus options as well.

After many days of research, Sameer came to the conclusion that it is best to start with a good device rather than upgrade later. Eventually, he bought a full-frame DSLR with a 50-megapixel sensor. He could print blow-ups if required. The device cost Rupees 175,000/- but, this was it. No more would he require any photographer or videographer's service. In fact, he would himself become a part-time photographer, he thought.

The camera got delivered on a Friday. Sameer was excited to get going with his new full-frame DSLR. So he spent the Friday evening unboxing the package and reading the manual. The next two days were for photography. He told Priya to dress up Myra and herself. They would be driving down to the Neemrana Fort on the Gurugram-Jaipur highway for a photoshoot. Sameer also planned to capture the sunset, landscapes, and much more on the trip.

Baby bags packed, the trip began at 9 am on Saturday. Lunch was at the Neemrana Fort. The entire day was spent clicking photos of Myra playing, Priya modelling, the fields, and the sunset. By the evening, some 500 photographs were clicked and reviewed on the LCD display. Priya put a lot of effort in posing the right way and handling Myra as well. The family returned at 8 pm. Tired, Priya put Myra to bed and retired herself as well. Sameer was excited to review his work. He pulled out the SD card and put it into the slot in his laptop. He was going to edit the pictures using the latest software available, which he planned to purchase just now. However, he thought to himself that he will review the pictures first.

The results were disappointing. Half of the pictures were blurred. Some were overexposed, some were too dark. Some were just right in everything, but the positioning of Myra or Priya in the picture frame was not correct. The pictures had seemed fine in the small LCD of the camera, but on a large display, the story was different. In total, about 95% of the photographs were unsuitable for prints or otherwise.

Sameer was unhappy with the results. He realized that having the best tools and the will to do something was not enough to do it well. If he needed to be a good photographer, he would have to spend hours and hours practising to become good at the settings of the device. It was as arduous and time-consuming to do photography, as it was to do risk management in finance.

Sameer thanked his stars that he was not himself clicking on Myra's birthday. Had those photographs been of this quality, he would have gotten an earful from his wife and in-laws, and the baby girl's special moments would have been permanently captured with poor skills. With this, he packed the camera in the bag and shelved it, where it lies to date. What happened with Sameer is something that happens to all of us in our financial lives as well.

DIY Investing

DIY or Do-It-Yourself is a mindset where you do not wish to pay for a service because you assume that either no one else has your best interest in mind, or that you can do it better than anyone else or you simply feel the service is too expensive for what it is worth. Consequently, you need to execute the service yourself. This is how Sameer thought about the photography service. He felt that he could do it better than the professional team because it was simple and easy. So he decided to try it out himself in order not to pay for the service in the future.

In our journey of helping people with their finances, we have come across a lot of DIY constructed portfolios. Most of these portfolios are remnants of investments made into the best-option-at-that-time products. These are highly complicated portfolios with lots of bits of knowledge splattered into them. These portfolios reflect concepts like goal-based investing, index investing, debt-equity glide-paths, value investing, and many other popular concepts marketed from time to time. The two consistent things we notice about such portfolios are:

A. They are very complex (not simple or sophisticated).

B. They are skewed to one type of asset class or strategy.

These portfolios are made with enthusiasm and then typically forgotten. Unfortunately, investment is a continuous process. If an investor wants to DIY, she needs to constantly monitor these investments and keep updating them from time to time. However, in our busy lives, the mundane task of monitoring gets ignored. Hence, layers and layers of complexity builds on.

The DIY Universe

With the advent of electronic trading, the skills to become a trader no longer required a loud voice, high energy levels, and a physical presence at the exchange. Electronic trading led to a drop in commissions charged as well. Barriers to entry in the profession got lowered. You only need a trading account, a DEMAT account, and some funds to start. So, a new kind of DIY market participant came about. The DIY trader.

DIY traders trade in various time frames - intra-day, end-of-day, few days, and even a few months. It is a well-known fact that most traders lose money, yet the lure of being the one odd guy who makes money is still there. Adding to this ease are the low cost, easy access to data, technical charting tools, trading consoles which look like a flight cockpit and accounts which open in a few clicks. Unfortunately, very few people are able to segregate portfolios between trading and investing. Their addiction to the short-term makes them neglect the long-term horizons of markets.

Another type of investors are the DIY stock pickers. In our experience, many such investors are MBAs and finance professionals. These investors feel that they have some special knack to pick great stocks from the plethora of choices available. Typically, they have some logic which is somewhat defined. Many stock pickers actually do pick great stocks.

There is no doubt about their skill. However, they tend to focus only on their picks. Investing is also about letting others work on your money so you can sit back and enjoy the returns. Stock pickers end up having concentrated portfolios, which lead to limited exposure of the markets. There are no best stocks. Stock market movements are made up of individual runs of a small group of stocks. There are no investors, advisors, or managers who can pick only winners at all times. DIY stock pickers eventually lose interest and end up with forgotten stocks in their portfolios, most of the time. If you observe carefully, you will find that there are thousands of books and literature on "*How to buy the best stocks,*" but hardly any on "*How and when to sell the stocks and book a profit.*" This is the story of DIY stock pickers actually.

Investment success is all about making money and not owning the best stock. Most DIY stock pickers get fascinated by good companies and assume that a good company is a good stock. This is a fundamental error. There are several gems of companies which give poor returns for a considerable length of time due to various reasons.

Next are the DIY fund selectors. Such investors have a general distrust in the financial salesperson. They are likely to have been ripped off in commissions and mis-sold complex instruments at some point of time in their financial journey, and they also realized that they were ripped off (Unfortunately, many investors never even find out they were ripped off). Typically, the rip off agents are part-time cross-seller of financial products, who themselves do not have knowledge of the products they are selling. So DIY fund selectors focus on choosing the best investment plans across a wide variety of investment products such as mutual funds, insurance, PMS, etc.

DIY fund selectors prefer to go direct to save distribution commission. If you talk to them, they often quote numerous studies which show how even a 0.5% commission saving per annum leads to large compounding differences in the long-term. It is indeed true that small commissions do make a significant difference in the long term returns. However, a professional distributor only makes a commission on the value of the client's corpus. In fact, it is in the interest of a full-time distributor to keep the client's portfolio value high at all times, with low volatility and smaller drawdowns. This would ensure that the distributor's commissions are always maintained. Practically speaking, a full-time distributor is actually incentivized to keep your corpus high. Regulations which limits or prohibits initial commissions help in this light too.

Good returns, in the long run, are not just about selecting the right fund. They are also dependent on asset allocation, tactical exposure change to an asset class as per its market cycle, and the counsel to stay put in turbulent times. Direct investors are not tactical experts and do not take into account the behavioural cost of their actions. These costs are very difficult to measure. In fact, it only makes sense to go direct if you are investing on the advice of a financial advisor (who charges a fee as well), or you really are an expert on the subject matter of fund evaluation and finance and have the time, the knowledge, and the energy to do it yourself. Reading a few search results on the internet does give you confidence, but it really is not a replacement for a good distributor or advisor.

Finally, there is the DIY goal seeker. Such investors set their goals and then pursue them relentlessly. They prefer to use low-cost instruments to invest. A typical instrument they use to participate in the stock markets is index funds. The objective is to keep on investing using low-cost and simple instruments until the target amount is met. Goal-based investing is a good way to invest. It is akin to putting on the blinders on the horse and keeping its focus away from unwanted distractions. However, two things work against DIY goal seekers.

Firstly, they tend to ignore market cycles. Indeed you should not time the markets, but some bit of allocation needs to be managed to keep the volatility of the portfolio low and attain the target amount on the desired date. By ignoring market cycles, the net rate of return can suffer greatly if the exit is at a low point.

Secondly, goal-based investing does not take into account the unexpected events of life. Events that have a deep impact on the finances of an investor typically derail them from their goals (more on this in chapter 27). Goal-based investing is good if you have lived through a good, long-run bull market. When markets underperform for longer periods, blind goal-based investing in a single asset class while ignoring cycles, and not planning for catastrophic liquidation events results in very poor outcomes. Goal-seeking is a relatively new concept. There is not much known about the long term outcomes of blind goal-seeking portfolios. This fact needs to be kept in mind.

Why do we DIY?

There are numerous reasons that tempt any individual to be a DIY investor. However, the primary reasons are lower cost and overconfidence. Let us look at the other reasons that cause the DIY mentality. Below is a list of conditions that are mostly present when an investor considers the DIY route of investing.

Internet Advice

The availability of simple explanations around a complex subject matter like finance and investing gives the investor a false confidence. After reading a few websites which give direct tips on performing better in the markets, or even quotes from famous and successful professional investors, most DIY investors feel a high degree of confidence in their investing abilities. The educated investor feels that he has read enough on the subject to know its nuances.

In the field of psychology, this is called the Dunning-Kruger effect. This means that people often mistakenly overestimate their ability and expertise more than it actually is. Alongside this, they underestimate others' abilities and expertise. This leads to an illusion of superiority. The DIY investors do not factor in their lack of experience in the field. They downplay the experience of others and feel that they can do it better themselves. However, the illusion evaporates over time with further experiences and knowledge. The graph looks similar to Figure 9:

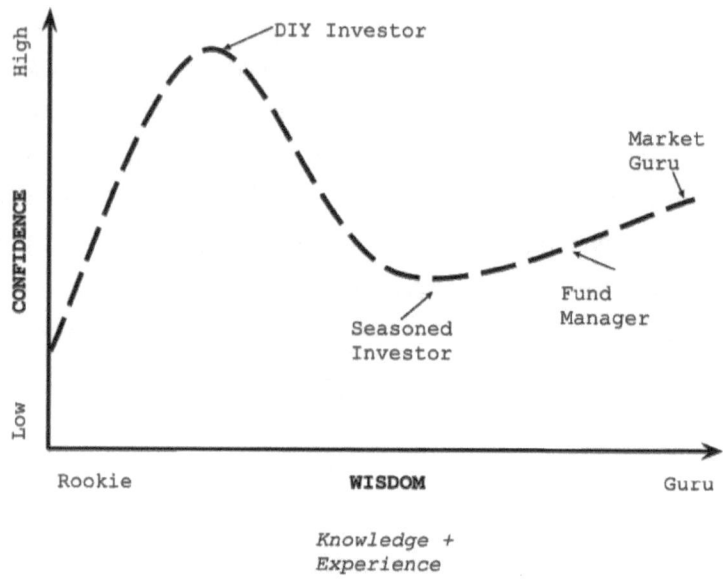

Figure 9: The Dunning-Kruger Effect in Investing

Cheap Information

Give enough data to a human brain, and it will start seeking patterns in it. If you open an online brokerage account, the broker is likely to provide you with a cockpit view of the markets. This plethora of indicators and data streams will make you feel like an expert to trade on your own.

In reality, you are as disadvantaged as the guy who checks stock prices on TV. Any sort of market data needs proper processing before it becomes useful information. A DIY investor simply lacks the tools to do this processing. After spending some time on random data, the human brain starts to find some patterns and start to believe in its ability to decode them. Over a longer period, it becomes comfortable with the data and starts to believe it is an expert in the matter. This phenomenon occurs because the human brain is susceptible to data addiction.

Further, the principle of GIGO - Garbage In, Garbage Out - also comes into play. For data to be informative, it has to be useful. Simply having access to a lot of data does not mean it is necessarily useful. If poor data is received by the human brain, it will only make poor decisions. Finally, with too much data, the human brain is also susceptible to information overload. This means too much information leads to poorer decisions (remember from Chapter 18, when making tough decisions, less is more).

The DIY investor is the most likely candidate to be lured by free data and supposedly free privileged information. Of course, privileged information is never free, but a one time offer does seem genuine to try out. Unfortunately, the DIY investor is also the most likely to be the conned candidate, through fake schemes and unscrupulous marketing.

Low Barrier to Access

The ease of access to a wide variety of financial contracts with low barriers to execution also supports the DIY mindset. This means that with a few clicks, you can quickly enter an investment - mutual funds, stocks, NCDs, bonds, IPOs, etc. In the digital age, ease of access is a boon. It saves effort, time, and money. However, access does not imply expertise.

A DIY investor feels empowered with this access. Yet they do not realize the consequences of this empowerment. We have often encountered individuals who have had success in one field, try to replicate the same in investing (remember overextending your expertise from Chapter 18). Like any other field, expertise in investing also takes time, practice, and survivorship.

Consider this, as an individual, if you fall sick, you seek a doctor; if you get into legal trouble, you seek a lawyer; if you want to file your tax returns, you seek the help of a chartered accountant. Each of these situations has a dire and foreseeable consequence if not taken care of. So we are likely to refer to a certified expert. Yet when it comes to investing, a lot of individuals prefer DIY.

This is partially due to the lack of understanding that finances and investment is an essential component of living today like health, tax, or the law. Playing with it is costly in the long run.

The second factor is the lack of foreseeable consequences of bad investing. This is called hyperbolic discounting. The utility of today's kick to DIY is greater than the utility to prevent a bad situation in the future. So with ease of access to DIY, an investor must consider their responsibility to her future self.

The DIY Disadvantage

The DIY gap has a huge cost to the investor. The DIY investor is at a disadvantage in comparison to a professional investor, or even the average investor (who invests through a fund manager or an advisor or a distributor). This is because a DIY investor is competing with a specialist, unknowingly. By virtue of having spent more time, having more experience, and also an information edge, the specialist performs better than the DIY investor, consistently.

At the same time, a DIY investor is working outside their circle of competence. Remember you are a specialist in only one area of your portfolio i.e., your job, profession, or business. The same is true for the DIY investor. He too is only an expert in his own field, but his biases or initial success or bad experiences with others makes him feel otherwise. The investment field is outside his circle of competence and thus he has the odds stacked against him.

Next, as a human being, the DIY investor is susceptible to loving the wins, not the money. We hear a lot of DIY investors talk about their right-calls over cocktails. Only later do we get to know that the winning amount was small, but the underlying losses from the bad calls were large. The objective of investment is to make money, not be right.

Finally, each time the DIY investor makes a decision and it works out well, he is at the risk of reinforcing wrong investing habits. Bad habits, when practised, set up the DIY investor for a big fail. Certain arts like driving a car or playing the guitar need initial guidance to have the right habits. For example, you always use the same foot to operate the accelerator and the brake of a manual transmission car. This is learnt. If a driver uses opposite feet, he may be effective in the initial stages but set for a crash in an exigent situation. Someone has to tell you that this is not to be done.

The DIY investing works just fine, till it does not. In times of crisis, the experience of a professional advisor or manager counts. Anyone can make money in a bull market. The DIY investor can too. The advisor or manager charges you a fee for saving you from bad markets, bad investments, and letting you make only the smaller mistakes.

An experienced distributor, a financial advisor or a fund manager, have value because they have been through the cycle and know how to handle extreme situations. Moreover, DIY portfolios become complex over time and lose relevance as life progresses. An external perspective then becomes important. You can DIY anytime, but at least now you know what is at stake.

Chapter 22

---❖---

The Limited Menu

The Phone Camera

Sameer's camera sits in storage to date. The only utility it provides Sameer is the satisfaction of having it. However, Sameer's Instagram account shows that he has become a good photographer. Equipped with only a phone, he clicks amazing shots! He only has to worry about how to compose them. The rest of the tweaking with the settings is done within seconds using the filters. Phone cameras have improved by leaps and bounds over the past few years. Yet they are nowhere close to the optical superiority Sameer's full-frame DSLR can give. Yet phones as cameras are a more popular choice than any DSLR in the market. It is not that they are better, but just more convenient.

Phones come with software which have preloaded and bundled settings. When the camera app is opened, the phone's software figures out the prevailing scenario. If it senses people's faces, it starts to identify them, if it is a sunset then appropriate settings are applied and so on for night photography, macros, motion, etc. All this is done with AI and data processing. Typically, the phone knows what settings to apply and suggests them as a bundle. It is hard to argue with the automatic settings. Next, when you post it on social media there are preset filter settings which create a certain effect. At that point, there are at most 1 or 2 settings that you can tinker with. You can get into the detailed settings and do more if you like. Finally, there is the text and frame that can be added as well. Lo and behold, you are ready to post in a few seconds.

In comparison to this, a DSLR photo needs to be loaded from the card to the laptop and then processed with individual settings. It is tiring and cumbersome and image manipulation requires expensive software as well. So, typically, the phone wins. It is not that the phone is really smart, but the phone manufacturers have figured what works best with humans - limited number of bundled choices.

Limited Choices

We, humans, are really bad at decision-making when the number of inputs in a decision increases. On the other hand, we are really good with A vs B choices. Some of us are better with A, B, and C choices. Beyond that, as the number of variables increases, so does the cognitive load. Phone makers know this. They understand that letting you tinker with individual settings can be fun, but the results will be poor. Over a longer period of time, you will get disinterested. So they bundle good settings together.

Decision-making also suffers when done in real-time. Our performance in making optimal decisions falls even further. Here, not worrying about individual settings really helps. Mostly, settings work well in certain configurations. If these configurations are preloaded, then you can focus on what the phone cannot do i.e., compose the picture. Investing is the same.

Investors are human beings. They too do not perform very well with too many choices. In the world of investing, there are more choices than there can be possible combinations to click a photograph. You can spend time to learn about these investment choices, but then you will probably be doing this only. If you are not a professional, full-time investor, too many investment choices can be confusing. You can make sub-optimal decisions and later face the consequences of having poorer finances available. Fortunately, you can follow at least one strategy each to reign in the human and financial perspectives. These will help you overcome the decision fatigue and choice overload of investing.

Prioritizing Goals

The first strategy is goal prioritization. Goals are the human perspective. Goals emanate from our wishes and desires. Some of these goals are essential, some are emotional, and some are aspirational. When the human mind focuses on a goal, it can overcome most obstacles in a way through hard work or innovation or facilitation. So, setting goals are effective in channelling energy or finances to reach them (with the help of advice, not DIY!).

Given the freedom, we can have many, many goals. Face it, not each one of us has all the finances to meet all goals that we can imagine. So it can be futile to try to fund all of these goals. Therefore, the goals need to be prioritized and trimmed to a few manageable ones. Doing this can be a tough exercise. However, Warren Buffet's 5/25 rule is a strategy which works very well here. You can list up to 25 of your goals, then spend time to prioritize them from 1 to 25. This can be done in many iterations and will take time. Once you have set an order, the top 5 on the list are the ones you really care about. These are the goals that need to be funded. The rest are distractions and will get in the way of the top five. The choice dilemma, which comes from the human perspective, can be reigned in using this exercise. Fewer goals are more likely to come to fruition.

Pre-determined Portfolios

The second strategy to follow is pre-determined portfolios. This strategy is used to reign in the financial perspective. Pre-determined portfolios are like bundled filters in a photo-sharing app. You can choose them and tweak them to your liking, yet you cannot go horribly wrong with the result. The most naive of these portfolios are debt-equity-gold asset allocation portfolios. Some of them look like this:

- Conservative - 60% Debt - 25% Equity - 10% Gold-Cash 5%
- Moderate - 50% Debt - 40% Equity - 5% Gold-Cash 5%
- Aggressive - 25% Debt - 65% Equity - 5% Gold- Cash 5%

We do not recommend any of the above classifications. These are for illustration purposes only. Yet, you cannot go horribly wrong with these portfolios. They are bundled choices which make you think about the human aspect of the problem i.e., your risk profile, and take care of the financial aspect i.e., asset allocation. These can be further tweaked as per the individual's needs.

Choosing the right bundle to start with can also be challenging. The one best suited for you is the one suggested by your financial advisor. A financial advisor can help you reduce the complexities of investing by helping you with your goal prioritization as well as portfolio selection.

FOBO Investing

FOBO is a term coined by *Patrick McGinnis*, a US venture capitalist who also coined the term FOMO (Fear Of Missing Out). FOBO stands for 'Fear of Better Option'. McGinnis defines the term as an obsessive research into every possible option when faced with a decision, leading to a paralysis when making a decision. This leads to indecision and regret.

When all the options have something better than the other, you may not be able to decide which one is the best. Humans are creatures of ranks and lists in terms of choice-making. When all options seem similar, humans cannot decide and get stressed. Consequently, they postpone the decision. This is a phenomenon different from inertia or the lack of change because the required research seems too heavy (as discussed in Chapter 17).

Try choosing a large cap mutual fund and you will experience a FOBO. There will be some attribute in each fund where it shines the best. Same is with debt or commercial properties or a designer for clothes! Even if you do make a tough choice between similar options, you can suffer from regret later that you could have done better. This is called buyer's remorse and may lead you to exercise the option to change. Such changes can be very expensive because they may incur transaction costs, contract breaking charges, and other expenses. FOBO investing is expensive and causes harm to the investor portfolios.

FOBO investing is the opposite of robo investing. When you go through a robo advisor, you have a limited set of options. You are given a pre-determined portfolio which is modified as per your requirements and preferences. All said and done, these options are not drastically different from the ones you started from. This is an advantage as well as disadvantage of robo investing. Robo investing does not allow you to do stupid things, yet it does try to fit one size to everyone by putting them into groups and types. Robo investing is a great way to overcome FOBO from a financial perspective. As an investor, your focus should be on the goals and outcome or the Human Perspective of money. The methodology can be left to the machines.

The Limited Menu Advantage

Humans are also susceptible to decision fatigue. This means if they are exposed to making decisions over and over again, they tire quickly and end up with bad choices. Limiting the menu of investing has certain advantages to overcome this fatigue. This can be done by knowing when and where to engage systems or strategies versus human beings when making decisions. Table 11 will help you compare situations.

Table 11: Systems, Strategies and Human skill use

	Systems	**Strategies**	**Humans**
Type of Decision to engage with.	High frequency decisions which are repetitive.	Nonlinear and complex decisions where a good amount of mathematics is involved or real time decision making is crucial or the options are too similar.	Abstract situations where A is not easily comparable to B and involves personal choices and preferences. These decisions can be assisted with math, but the final choice is human dependent.
Daily Life Example	What to eat for breakfast every day! (On of the authors has eggs, toast and tea every day for breakfast)	Which Large Cap mutual fund to buy.	Whether to fund the purchase of a car or a vacation to Japan in the next 5 years.
Finance Example	Execution decisions made by an algorithm for an Arbitrage Fund.	Stock Selection, Market Direction and Asset Allocation.	Capital Allocation to goals.
Finance Expert	Execution Algorithm	Fund Manager or Strategic Algorithm	You, the investor.

By limiting ourselves to only abstract decisions, a lot of good choices can be made with positive outcomes. As an investor, you should remember that just because you have access to the cockpit (of an investing platform's dashboard), does not mean you can fly the airplane. You should leave the lower level settings to well-researched algorithms. Let the asset allocation be the domain of a fund manager or a robo advisory algorithm. Finally, as an investor, you should discuss your goals with an advisor and figure them out. Those are your personal decisions.

PART 5

Finer Things My MBA Did Not Teach ME

Chapter 23

Don't Use a Hammer Where a Screwdriver is Required

Going to the Hospital

Sameer's father, Mr Sherawat, has been complaining about his eyesight. He has told Sameer that he is not able to read the screen of his phone clearly. Mr Sehrawat already uses reading glasses. The prescription was updated a few months ago. This worries Sameer. Could there be some other trouble with his father's health? He could have blood pressure issues, or diabetes, or perhaps some other complication with his eye. After discussion with Priya, they decide to take their father to the nearby hospital.

At the hospital, the general physician performs a thorough checkup. He notes the blood pressure of Mr Sehrawat. It is a bit over the limit. So he tries to understand whether Mr Sehrawat smokes or drinks or has any specific dietary habits. The answer is negative. Mrs Sehrawat keeps insisting that there is nothing wrong with him other than that he can't read properly. However, Sameer keeps insisting that the eye prescription for the reading glasses was only updated some months ago. Since he is having some trouble, it could be anything. The whole day passes by with a battery of tests being performed. At the end of the day, there is nothing serious found that needs to be acted upon. The physician is satisfied and gives an all-okay report. In the end, he suggests that it would be best if Sameer refers his father to the eye department as well. Since the OPD hours have finished, they would have to come the next day.

The next day Sameer takes his father to the hospital again. There, at the eye department, he meets a young doctor heading the department. Just after his residency is over, the doctor has been tasked with assembling the team for the eye department. The hospital is procuring equipment as the team is building up for specific examinations and procedures. Sameer gets his father's eye examined. After dilating the pupils and using different refractive scopes, the doctor concludes that his father has a cataract setting in his eyes. While the eye is okay, he will still need a procedure to remove the cataract. He suggests that they perform surgery to relieve his father of the discomfort. Sameer agrees. Mr Sehrawat is not so sure. So they head home to give it a thought for a few days.

In the evening, Sameer sits with his father after dinner to discuss why he is reluctant to get the surgery done. Mr Sehrawat is sitting comfortably on the sofa. With a cup of hot milk in his hand he replies in his buoyant voice, "Sammy, tell me, would you use a hammer to drive a screw inside a piece of furniture? And would you hire a plumber for the very task?"

Sameer is confused with his father's questions. He inquires what's on his mind. His father explains that while Sameer was being counselled by the eye doctor in the doctor's cabin, he was waiting outside. During this time, he walked up to the reception area and started a friendly chat with the nurse at the station. He got two vital pieces of information from her.

Firstly, the hospital's eye department was new. They did have the equipment to perform a cataract surgery but it was not the latest technology and procedure. It did do the job, however, there was a better procedure available, just not at this hospital. Secondly, the doctor he was consulting was a retinologist. This procedure pertained to the cornea. The cornea expert was a visiting doctor. So far the hospital had changed 3 of these visiting doctors. It wasn't that the hospital did not know what it was doing, it was just that there was a better procedure and a better expert available elsewhere. In fact, what they should do is to find an eye speciality hospital and get a second opinion.

Sameer is surprised at his father's information gathering skills and then piecing it together into a fluid logic. He wonders how good a financial analyst he would have made. He agrees with him. He realizes that his good experience with the hospital during Myra's delivery and his mother's bypass surgery had made him overlook some key aspects of this particular case.

There is No One-Stop-Shop

Every hospital is not equipped with each and every speciality. In Mr Sehrawat and Sameer's case, the trusted hospital was not really well equipped with the ophthalmology department. They were building it, but it was not ready as of yet. This is true in finance as well. We often meet investors who have used one single mutual fund asset management company (AMC) to invest all their funds into the market. They simply believe in the AMC's capabilities and justify their action by citing past results, the size of the AMC, and other factors like the age of the AMC and its presence.

We thoroughly disagree with this investing approach. Trust is important in financial investing, however, it is not the only criteria to invest. Just because an AMC has a wide variety of fund schemes available in its portfolio of schemes, it doesn't mean that all the schemes are performing well.

A scheme is operated by its fund manager. In a discretionary scheme, the fund manager's capabilities matter a lot. This means different schemes with the same fund house would perform differently. As an investor, if you wish to get exposed to different types of risks-return profiles in your portfolio, you would be doing yourself a disservice by investing in schemes which belong to only a particular fund house. The only exception to this would be algorithmically run quantitative schemes, which have a validated backtest or live performance track record. Other than that, putting all your money in a single AMC exposes you to something called AMC risk. There have been instances where a large AMC has failed in one scheme and the risk has cascaded to other schemes. Simply put, trust in an AMC is good, but putting all your money in a single AMC is an over-extension of that trust. The lure of a one-click portfolio is great, but an oversimplification is not the right investment approach.

There is No Single Winning Strategy

As an investor, you should also be aware that there is no one strategy which wins all the time. This means certain strategies will perform well in certain market conditions, while others will perform better in a different set of conditions. This is akin to having the right specialist for the right job. If a retinologist would be expected to perform the task of a cornea specialist, there is a likelihood that he will not perform so well or perhaps not be able to perform at all!

The most common fallacy we observe with investors is the use of a value strategy. A value strategy means that a stock or portfolio of stocks is cheaper relative to its actual book value. This means it is at a bargain price. However, a stock being offered at a bargain price is relative to the market conditions as well. In a beaten market, when all stocks are depressed, a stock with good fundamentals is a bargain temporarily. We know that markets do not stay beat up forever. When the market recovers, the stock with good fundamentals recovers quickly and yields great gains.

However, this is not true in a converse scenario. When the market is good, and a stock is beaten exclusively, it is not a value pick! There must be information regarding the stock which is being factored in its price, which may not be publicly available as yet. Being a value investor in such cases does not pay off. In fact, stocks which lose more than 50% of their value do not recover 95% of the time, even if their fundamental ratios say otherwise. We know loads of investors who have fundamental gems in their portfolios, but they have not budged over the past many years.

Contrasting in philosophy to a value strategy is a growth strategy. Growth stocks beat the market in a bull run. They move higher and higher on their future prospects. However, they do not beat the market in a bear market. When market sentiment goes sour, all future prospects seem bleak. Growth stocks fall faster than other stocks in such markets. So you cannot go all-in on a growth strategy and expect it to perform all the time!

The third popular approach is the contrarian strategy. This means you deploy money into investment themes and ideas which are not doing well presently, but are likely to (hope) do better in the future. The success of a contrarian strategy lies in timing the markets. If you do not time the markets with contrarian themes, you will get a good percentage return (eventually) but a poor CAGR. This is because the theme may not perform for a long time and you will be stuck with duds. 99% of investors fail at timing markets. So, as a standalone approach to portfolio, a contrarian strategy is risky as well.

Portfolio of Strategies

Relying on a single investment strategy can be expensive. It is a knowledge gap as well as a behavioural gap. Investors may not know that other good strategies exist or are too confident about the one they are familiar with. So what should be the right approach? The simplest solution is to use many experts (strategies). Instead of building a portfolio of stocks, you should build a portfolio of investment strategies, AMCs, and management styles. Here is a map to go by in order to diversify an equity portfolio (Table 12 is not exhaustive and can be defined in many other ways).

Table 12: Portfolio of Strategies

Fundamental Strategies	Growth
	Value
	Contrarian
Quantitative Strategies	Trend Following/Counter-Trend
	Statistical Arbitrage/Convertible Arbitrage and Fixed Income Arbitrage
	Spreads
	Global Macro
Technical Strategies	Price Patterns
	Price Transform Indicators
Fund Management Styles	Discretionary
	Algorithmic
	Quantamental

By building yourself a portfolio of investment strategies, you will be able to get good returns in a systematic way. Any investment strategy will beat the market at some point in time but not always. This approach emphasizes the fact that your agenda is good returns to meet your goals, not beating the market.

Chapter 24

Read the Fine Print

The Statement

Mrs and Mr Sehrawat are in Mumbai visiting their younger son and daughter-in-law. Sumit is super happy when his father is around. It means he can be the carefree child of the house again. It is a relief for Poorni as well because her mother-in-law cooks well and they get delighted with a great menu every day! Mr Sehrawat likes the responsibility too. When he is in Mumbai, he takes care of running the house. One of his responsibilities is to ensure that all bills are paid on time by Sumit and Poorni.

The mail arrives and Mr Sehrawat comes across the credit card bill of his son. He opens and has a look into the statement. The items are usual, movie tickets, groceries, restaurant bills, etc. Except for the last 3 items. An EMI instalment of INR 18,500 per month, a late fee of INR 500, and an interest charge of INR 555 plus taxes, and previous dues of an unpaid instalment of INR 18,500. Mr Sehrawat's heart sinks. He had taught his sons better about debt and one of them was headed in the wrong direction. He calls up Sameer and explains the matter to him. Sumit is using revolving credit to fund some things, and, on top of it, his home loan's EMI is also due. Sameer tries to calm him down.

The C-Debt

The world around us today is designed to get us into debt. Go online to an e-tailer website and select items in your shopping cart. When you proceed to checkout, the first click is the "buy now" button. Next is the payment mode with a "By Credit Card" option. Then you get prompted to "Pay in EMIs" with 3 or 6 or 12 months options. Finally, the OTP comes through an SMS message. Within a span of 45 seconds, the cost of today's purchase is pushed into the future with an EMI.

If you notice carefully, you will see that you only get to see the EMI and not the total cost you will pay including interest. The credit card company banks on the fact that you will not multiply the EMI cost with the number of EMIs and subtract the total with the actual cost of the purchase. This will show you a figure of what extra you are going to pay. If you divide it with the actual cost, you will see the extra percentage of money you are going to pay to buy the same thing. Not showing the total cost is not illegal. Instead, for the total figure, a derivative of that figure is shown. This is a figure you can comfortably come to terms with.

On the other hand, if the "buy now" button was replaced with "Pay Now," would it prompt you to make a purchase? Also, if the EMI options displayed the total and excess you would need to pay over the actual cost, would you opt for EMI? Probably not! It would be equivalent to telling you what you can or can't afford. Therefore, by design, it is convenient for us to get in debt for non-essential things. Simply put, in today's world, debt is convenient.

The P-Debt

Now, consider a medical emergency, a vacation to blow steam and to avoid a burnout, a pressing payment, a family member's request for assistance, a social celebration, a child's demand, or a spouse's nag. These situations can create stress and we get motivated to relieve it. The easiest option available to get relief is debt in the form of a personal loan. The personal loan is a great therapist, it simply does not ask for what the problem is, it just obliges with instant relief. However, this relief comes at a cost that often becomes a painful experience later on. Personal loans are the second most costly debt options after credit card loans.

The convenience and relief debt offers are not enough. The ease at which you can get it is a top-up factor. The general rule of thumb is,

"The easier it is to get debt, the costlier the debt is."

Once you have taken debt in your life, you have a credit score. If you pay it up, it improves and you are offered even more debt. Your bank, your credit card company and NBFCs will keep pinging you with offers. They congratulate you for the good score you have and flash attractive rates you will get at the click of a button and no documents required. The bombardment is so heavy that at some point in time, you are likely to cave in when you are still making up your mind about the need to finance something. Taking up debt once makes it easy to get debt again. The ease is addictive.

So the convenience debt offers, the relief it gives, and ease at which you can get debt, are the three basic things designed to get you in debt. But debt has a cost, which is not just the interest rate. It has a physical, emotional, and mental cost as well.

The Fine Print

What is that you do when you purchase something on EMI? Two basic things:
1. You pre-pone the purchase of something you cannot afford now.
2. You are adjusting it against your future income.

Technically, this is equivalent to spending more than you earn. Or, in simpler terms, living beyond your means. Behaviourally, it is very difficult for the brain to accept the fact that you cannot afford something you want. So the brain looks for a solution. It justifies that you should just borrow to fill in the gap. The brain also gets a temporary high from the immediate gratification. This high blocks its ability to see the future consequences of the actions done to fulfil the desires of the present. Once done, it starts looking for the next high.

Debt offers a temporary increase in your purchasing power. You can afford to buy what you want now, paying it off over time from future earnings. However, it's important to understand that the downside of this approach is that your future earnings are now going to be spread much thinner.

Now, say in the future, a minor shock or even a Black Swan event comes in and disturbs your income stream. The income is not there or is lower than before. However, the EMI does not care about this. It needs to be serviced. If you are unable to do it, you need to borrow some more to service the existing debt. This loss of income will also affect your lifestyle. Now suddenly you need to borrow even more to maintain your lifestyle. However, the problem does not end there. The more debt you have, the more you are likely to have. The term for this is debt spiral. It is a situation in which an individual, or business, or nation, sees ever-increasing levels of debt to fund the servicing of existing debt. These increasing levels of debt and interest and incidental charges to be paid on debt becomes unsustainable, eventually leading to debt default.

Warren Buffet says,

> *"If you buy things you don't need,*
> *you will soon have to sell things you need."*

If you tend to splurge, this is a great line to memorize and repeat to stop yourself when you feel compelled to reach for a totally unnecessary item in the store or hit the "buy now" button on your computer.

The second thing your brain does not realize at the moment when you are taking debt is that some part of your income is going to pay interest on the principal that was borrowed. For most people, it's hard to comprehend just how expensive this can be. As your credit card debt increases, your interest costs and minimum payment requirements rise. If your income isn't increasing, interest begins to consume a larger and larger percentage of your monthly take-home income. This makes you even more dependent on credit to get by. This is called credit creep.

Once credit creep sets in, it keeps on swallowing more and more of your income, making lesser and lesser of it available to you. At this stage, your brain will not remember the previous actions that cause this situation. The brain will only revolt and curse the debt. In the case of companies and nations in such a situation, the next management or government only seeks a bailout. Unfortunately, individuals are not bailed out.

In order to avoid credit creep, you may have to cut on your lifestyle. However, lifestyles are formed out of habits. So now you have one set of habits, which are lifestyle, competing with a second set of habits, which are instant gratification. This is a bad situation to be in.

Deleveraging

Debt also amplifies the negatives in your life. A mortgaged home limits your mobility. It weighs on your mindset and may prevent you from taking up better opportunities in another city. On top of that, you may not be able to sell the house because of the lock-ins of time and price by the financing institution.

In case you do decide to sell and are permitted to, the psychological damage of a distressed sale is immense. This damage is further amplified by the financial hit you may take by selling at a low price.

Missing debt payments has a cost too - a hit on the credit score. This means any future debt may not be available to you or may be available at a higher cost and interest rates. Leverage has more negative effects than positive.

The only way to not spend beyond your means, not surrendering your choices, not marginalizing your lifestyle, not hurting your psychology, not limiting your mobility, and not overpaying for things, is to not take debt. If you have debt, start paying it off as soon as possible. As a rule, pay the most expensive debt first. Alternately, pay off the lenders to whom you owe a smaller amount first. This way you have fewer parties to deal with. This plan should be made and implemented with the help of a financial advisor or a banker.

In order to finish debt, you may have to take drastic steps. This means you may have to sell an asset, reduce your lifestyle expenses, cancel a holiday, or all of them and more. Do whatever it takes.

The Two Step Debt Strategy

Debt is a tool for leverage, it should be engaged when the following two conditions are met:

1. You have a constant cash flow that covers the outflow from the debt servicing.
2. When you are funding an investment and not a purchase.

Condition number 1 is easy to understand. It means that if you do not have a secure, regular income, you are not a qualified candidate for taking debt. This implies that if you are a professional, a business owner, or a freelancer and you do not have secured active or passive income then you should avoid debt. If your income gets disturbed or varies for even a short period of time, then you are likely to experience debt spiral and/or credit creep. Only if you have a stable active or passive income should you consider debt. Your assets need to pay for your liabilities. From a long term perspective, there is no secure income. Everything gets disturbed at some point in time. More of that to be understood in Chapter 27.

The second condition means that you should only finance something with debt when it has an appreciating value. To make this clear consider the following examples.

Good use:

- Buying a house using debt while living in it as well, provided you have a regular cash flow of passive income or a secure job. The value of the house will increase eventually.

- Investing in a solar farm using debt with a secured contract from the power distribution company to buy power at a minimum rate for the tenure of the debt. The earnings from selling the power output of the farm will cover the cost of the asset.

Bad use:

- Buying an expensive car on debt. As the novelty and utility of the car wears off, the debt becomes painful and the owner may soon be looking for a buyer.
- Debt used to purchase and renovate a bread and breakfast facility. Given the facility looks like a 5-star hotel, the booking rates would be high in good times (when people travel). However, in case the demand drops (like it did during the COVID-19) crisis, servicing the debt becomes a pain.

A Note on Appreciating Assets

We want to specially mention what people think about appreciating assets when taking debt. An appreciating asset is a contextual case. We know a lot of people who bought commercial properties by down paying only 30-40% of the cost. Their plan was to finance the rest and use the rent to pay the EMI. During the Covid-19 pandemic, an exceptional circumstance happened - the rent stopped. Yet, the EMIs continued (even with moratorium) and the corpus put up as margin got eroded due to fall in the value of the commercial property. Commercial properties were considered a sure-shot appreciating asset. This belief too was tested.

We do not recommend taking debt. Nevertheless, if you still need to take on debt, here are three quick rules of thumb to remember:

RULE #01: The longer the tenure of the debt, the higher is the amount you will pay over the original cost of the item.

RULE #02: The easier it is to get the debt, the higher will be its cost (interest rate, processing fee).

RULE #03: All fancy features (Balloon Payments, Pre-EMI, moratorium, etc.) are an extra cost, there is nothing free.

Alternatives to Debt

So if you want it, but cannot afford it, how to go about it? The answer to this is:

"Defer it."

Be your own financer. Set yourself a target date and figure the amount you can put in per month to finance it. This will help you determine the rate of compounding that is required to meet the target. Once the rate has been determined, you will need to figure what asset classes and instruments to use to get there. This typically requires some financial knowledge and you are likely to need the help of a financial advisor. Converting the EMI to a SIP helps accumulate the required corpus to purchase a liability without getting leveraged in the process. As a result, you keep your freedom, do not pay more than the actual cost of the purchase, and stay happier. Studies show that people without debt are a lot happier than those with it.

Chapter 25

———✦———

Preparing for Entrepreneurship

The Banker's Leap to Enterprise

Sameer has an idea. It has occupied space in his head for a while. Then it came down to paper. Now, it is being discussed in words and being expressed as intention. Sameer's friends, who work in venture capital funds, have given him a thumbs up regarding the idea. Fintech is the buzzword. Sameer has a fintech idea which is scalable. Along with the scalable idea, Sameer has a good profile with great antecedents, the right maturity, and ability to lead good teams. These are key to doing a business and being funded by a VC.

At home, Sameer has been hinting to Priya regarding starting his own venture. She has not responded with much other than "Okay" and "Umhmmm." So Sameer is not sure whether she is fully receptive to the idea or not. He wants Priya's buy-in into the whole concept before they proceed.

On a Tuesday evening, after putting Myra to bed, he sits down with Priya to discuss. He tells her that he wants to promote a start-up. Priya smiles, as if she already knew what was coming. She gives Sameer a hug and tells him, "I am very happy for the both of us!" Sameer is both relieved and confused. She adds, "But! There is one condition." Sameer raises a brow. He knew something was coming. "You will have to meet Rahul and discuss this through. Not the business idea. That, I have no doubt you have thought out well. But what about all that comes along with leaving a job and starting a business. Rahul has been through ups and downs as an entrepreneur. Let's get his mind on this too." Sameer agrees. He sees the merit in Priya's argument. So he immediately calls up Rahul and fixes up a one-on-one for the coming Sunday at a local microbrewery in Gurugram.

Entrepreneurship 101

Sunday noon is a busy time at the microbrewery. Sameer arrives ten minutes before time and finds a table. The tables around his own are abuzz. He can figure there are friends meeting after a long time, a few young professional people debating the latest policies, and some even discussing a start-up idea. Rahul arrives on time. They shake hands and order their beers.

Rahul directly gets to the point. He asks Sameer about his idea. Sameer explains to him the fintech setup which runs around education, training, and investment services in finance. Rahul patiently listens and nods. After a while, Rahul tells Sameer that he likes his idea and does see the merit and potential in it. However, he adds that it's not just the idea, or the team, or the funding or the timing which matters in the success of a start-up. It is the mindset which matters the most. The setup of the entrepreneur counts as well. Sameer is intrigued. He asks Rahul to explain.

Rahul explains, "See Sameer, being an entrepreneur is a commitment. Most people who decide to be an entrepreneur do have a mental commitment. However, the game is not just in the mind. You have to prepare physically to be able to succeed as an entrepreneur. Let me tell you what this means. I will discuss some pointers and you can note the responses on your phone. By the end of this conversation, you yourself will have the answer as to whether you are ready or not. No need to tell me about your responses. Okay?" Sameer agrees and Rahul begins.

Rahul continues, "Okay so I hope you are clear with the reasons why you want to do the business. It could be that you want to make money or perhaps you want to change the way something works in the world or you may be passionate about an idea and a dream you want to follow. That is okay, but before you make the world a better place for everyone, the first thing you need to do is to be able to take care of yourself to make that change. This means you have to be able to take care of the people dependent on you, meet your obligations, and have a normal life in due course of building a business. So figure out how you are meeting these requirements for now. If it is through the income which comes from a job, then this income needs to be replaced first or saved to be used later. I would recommend that you should have 36 months covered. It is a lot of time. But believe me, a business will take some time to take off. Meanwhile, food in the stomach is as important as fire in the belly."

He summarizes, "So the first thing is to compute your current obligations, including that of your dependents, household expenses, etc. and see how they will be covered for the next 36 months. This could be either through the income Priya earns, once she gets back to work, or some other source like rentals or interest or through savings." Sameer nods and sees the logic in Rahul's argument.

Rahul adds, "The other important thing is that you should not be in debt of any sort before you take up the start-up route. See, businesses give income or returns when they come of age, not when you want them to or need them to. Having the burden of debt will distort your thinking in tough times while starting up. The returns from the business will take some time to stabilize. Whereas the servicing of debt will be a constant. I will not suggest that you get into a situation where a constant requirement ends up being serviced by a variable source. It is a bad fix to be in. It will affect your long term thinking and keep you focussed on the short term only. That can be detrimental for both you and the family, and for the business. So consider the debt situation." Sameer notes diligently.

"Finally, one more thing I would like to suggest," Rahul says, "Ask yourself about your lifestyle."

"What about it?" asks Sameer.

Rahul replies, "See, I know you do not live a lavish lifestyle. You guys are in control. Frankly, Priya and you live more modestly than most young people of your age with incomes around your range. That is good. However, entrepreneurship is a long game, it does see ups and down from time to time. The way to smoothen those times is to control your expenses. Now do not get me wrong when I say anything about controlling your expenses. I do not intend to say that you should not enjoy your coffee at the cafe of your choice or not watch online TV or trim your internet bill. What I mean to say is that, look at the larger heads of lifestyle expenses. Try to shrink these expenses before you start the enterprise journey. This is because when the income stops from the job and business requires money, the heat will be on for some time. Downsizing lifestyle at that point in time becomes difficult. It is like fighting a war on multiple fronts. You can win on all fronts. Any loss means game over. Also, at that point in time, you may be motivated to cut down lifestyle, but others in the family may not be so responsive and it will create undue distress. Both the sisters, Priya and Kirti, are supportive girls. I know because Kirti has been with me through thick and thin and never once complained. You are lucky you have Priya. She has the same good values. But why push them at that point in time."

"The best way," Rahul adds, "is to start doing it now. One by one, step by step. A twenty percent reduction means you can last five months on the same budget instead of four. That is a big deal!" Sameer notes down and reflects within.

Entrepreneurship 201

"The next set of factors that come into picture are related to the mindset of doing the business," says Rahul. "From my experience, I have observed that most people who jump from doing a job to doing a business or scaling a small enterprise to a large scale setup, are hesitant to share ownership. They feel since they are doing the hard work, they should get most of the reward. So they do not like to give equity."

He continues, "I am sure since you are going to approach a VC for funding, you may not be thinking like this. However, let me caution you against the misuse of the other option than giving equity. It is debt. In its most basic form, debt is leverage. This means if you have 1 rupee of your own, then you can borrow say 2 more rupees to work with, provided you give back 3 in the long run. This works well for a business which already has a cash flow. It can start paying back the debt immediately and still earn more than the interest paid towards the debt. This way the ownership of the business remains the same, undiluted."

"But," adds Rahul, "a start-up like yours is not an established business. It does not have a cash flow setup for now. By God's grace, it will, in due time. So you cannot or should not take debt to start the business. In fact, the debt you will most likely have to take will be a personal loan. This is the most expensive sort of debt that you can get out there. Do not fall into that trap. Always remember debt is an expensive employee."

"On the other hand," explains Rahul, "equity is a pushing partner. Anyone who has put equity into your start-up is a partner. They have not just put in money, but also shown you the commitment to be there with you for the success of the venture. They shall also bring in their domain expertise and complement your skill set. Selection of a VC partner may also include the consideration of the network that he will give you access to. The flip side, or perhaps not, is that you have to give them equity in your business. But come to think of it, would you rather have 100% share of Rs. 100 or 50% share of Rs. 500?"

"The second one is obvious," replies Sameer. He adds, "There is always more prospect in scale and the scope increases too."

"Yes!" replies Rahul, "Not only does the scale and scope increase, but so does the diversification of the entrepreneur, his chances to survive and thus to make the business a success. Even if the entrepreneur has the Rs. 1,000 required for the business, it still makes sense for him to share the risk with others. Risk works both ways, upside and downside. The entrepreneur who has the sense of both directions of outcomes will always invite equity into his venture. This way he can spend, say Rs. 500 on the business and invest Rs. 500 elsewhere. Trust me, this is how it worked for me! Though I wasn't so thoughtful about it. Someone else was. I am grateful to him for his advice."

Entrepreneurship 301

"Finally, Sameer, there is also the possibility of things not working out as planned. It is also an important aspect to consider at the very beginning only," notes Rahul. He continues, "See it is not that you have to be a pessimist or a realist, but preparing for a negative outcome reduces the anxiety. It will help you perform better in low times as well. It is an important aspect of managing your psychology."

"In this aspect ask yourself 'what if it all doesn't work out?' By answering this you will know what other things you can do. It will make you think of a plan B, plan C, and even plan D. For a venture capitalist, this is an important aspect too. It is called flight risk. By assessing the flight risk, a VC will know how safe his investment is. This comes with preparing for losing. There is a known Silicon Valley adage which says,

"Fail fast, and fail cheap."

Sameer looks up and replies, "This is an aspect I really have not considered. Thank you for bringing it up."

"Yes," adds Rahul, "it is not wrong to lose. However, it should not be a debilitating blow to your mind and career. Your business plan should also contain a section, for only yourself, a contingency plan in case of a loss. Often planning for losing outcomes, brings in the grit required for success. See failure is not an option, however, losing is a part of the game. When you define failure, you will get up each time you lose because you will not be afraid of it."

He adds, "Sometimes things do not work out at all. In fact, at times it is smart to quit. As the famous *Paulo Coelho* has said,

*"If you are brave enough to say goodbye,
life will reward you with a new hello."*

Quitting is not failure if it is the best option. It should not define you as a person. There is a big difference between giving up and knowing when enough is enough. Also, a venture not working out should not end up destroying you financially. It should be a calculated risk. So do keep these factors in mind." Sameer notes.

Sameer summarizes, "I think it also means that I should keep my channels open to come back to a job respectfully in case things do not work out. Also, more importantly, I should consider an exit strategy in case I am not able to make it. Wow! Thank you for the point, Rahul. I feel much more confident now." Mentally, he thanks Priya for the push.

Chapter 26

The Myth of Retirement

The Myth

Human life is finite and so are all its parts. Childhood is finite, youth is finite, and so are our working lives. Even our scriptures talk about a stage of life, "*Vanaprastha*" (Retirement) where the individual moves after "*Grahasthya*" (Family Life) and before the stage of "*Sanyasin*" (Renunciation). Even before our career begins, we understand that one day we will stop working and retire. Retirement is a concept ingrained in our society initially by design and presently by belief.

When retirement is far, there is a hope that somehow things will all fall into place and be taken care of. A few years later, you start to envisage the second-order effects that happen with retirement. You understand that your active income will stop because you will stop working. Then if you have saved well, you will be able to either consume those savings as a pension, or regularly dip into a retirement fund, or somehow generate income from those savings in the form of an annuity to sustain your lifestyle.

A few more years later, you will start to understand that there can also be unforeseen expenses for you and your loved ones for health and other emergencies. Perhaps these you have not provisioned for presently. As time passes by and retirement comes nearer, the picture starts to become more clear. You get to know where you are likely to land at the end of your career and start planning to adjust your lifestyle accordingly.

Retirement is an important phase of life. Countless people have retired since the industrial age began (where the concept was originally formed and average human lifespan was shorter than the retirement age), and countless will still retire. Talking about retirement triggers intense feelings. You may feel relieved if you do not really like what you do, or feel liberated because you will have the time to do only those things that you like, or even feel confused because you do not know what you will do afterwards. These feelings are the human perspectives of retirement.

The financial perspective just boils down to one question: How much money do I need to retire comfortably? This is one question which has bogged down everyone. There are volumes written on the subject, but there is no definitive answer from the academics or from the financial industry. When the financial perspective doesn't answer a question, the human perspective builds a proxy answer. There are theories and lore around what is the best strategy for retirement. These strategies vary from mathematical models to special secret tactics. Planning for retirement is hard and the possibility of negative consequences is real.

When humans think of the future, they never see negative outcomes for themselves. They feel that if some negative eventuality has a remote possibility of happening to only a small percent of the population, then they would be ones who will be saved from it. This is called possibility effect. That is why we build stories which have happy endings. These myths serve our imagination and give us hope. Retirement is one such myth where everything supposedly ends well and we shall live happily ever after.

Why is Retirement Hard?

Retirement is far away when you start. An event which is 40 years away is difficult to plan for now, especially when there are more urgent and pressing things on the way. Even if you plan for things now, the actual conditions then will be much different. There will be social, economic, and technological changes which may make the plans of today redundant 40 years in the future.

If that was not enough, on the way to planning this event there will be many unforeseen surprising and upsetting events. These events will accelerate or decelerate your pace and distract you from your retirement plans. Some events may even completely detract you from your path, because of the urgency they pose, making you look away from the future.

The unknown options and fuzzy outcomes make retirement a tough thing to contemplate and plan for (Remember Chapter 18). The Nobel Laureate economist Bill Sharpe says,

"Knowing how to strike a balance between having enough income to meet your current needs and having enough to get you through your lifetime, is the nastiest, hardest problem in finance."

Consequently, retirement planning gets put off. Most people only seriously start to think about retirement in their late 30s if not 40s or 50s, when they are forced to. It means going to a financial planner and setting priorities in order. Then building a financial plan around this and acting upon it.

There are various mathematical formulas and plans for retirement that can be followed. Most involve your expenses today, the rate of inflation, compensation for known pitfalls, and selecting the right instruments. The retirement computations involve the following stages as shown in Table 13:

Table 13: Assumptions in Retirement Planning

Present Values>>	Assumptions>>	Future Value
1. Your current monthly expenses.	1. The stability of Real rate of Returns (Accounting for Inflation).	1. Your future monthly expenses.
2. Your current monthly income.	2. The stability of Direct and Indirect Taxes.	2. Your post-retirement goals.
3. Your present total Savings/Investments.	3. Continuity and Growth rate of your income.	
	4. Number of years in retirement.	
	5. Known contingencies - like health and a factor for unknown contingencies.	
	6. Growth in your lifestyle.	

Planning for retirement is tough because there are too many assumptions. Most formulas will focus on Column 1 (Present values) and assume average values for Column 2 (Assumptions) to compute Column 3 (Future values). The challenge lies in Column 2. There are 6 assumptions listed and there are perhaps many more. Unfortunately, none of the 6 assumptions are under our control (except for growth in lifestyle). Any small misestimation in any of these values can lead to compounded and irreversible errors. This is the catch in retirement planning. Even assuming a factor of safety in computing these values does not necessarily insulate us from the effect of miscalculations (Factor of safety is a linear variable. However, rates of return and time have non-linear effects in the compounding formula).

From these formulas, some retirement cults have sprouted. One such cult is F.I.R.E.

F.I.R.E.

An aggressive strategy for retirement which is popular amongst the millennials is F.I.R.E. - Financially Independent, Retire Early. Proponents of the F.I.R.E. strategy believe that if they can save enough and save hard early on in their careers, they can retire early. Early means sometime as soon as the 40s. The goal for the F.I.R.E. followers is financial independence. They do not intend to have more wealth than they can spend, but just enough to last a lifetime. The objective is to live the best life with the least amount of money required. The F.I.R.E. movement originated with the classic, *Your Money or Your Life* by *Vicki Robin and Joe Dominguez*. The book inspires millennials to change their relationship with money, live deliberately, spend mindfully, eliminate debt, save early, and build wealth.

F.I.R.E. aficionados estimate that *"once your net worth is 25 times your annual expenses, you've achieved financial independence."* There is a debate whether the right amount is 25x or 30x or 40x or more. Given you do not know how the 6 variable assumptions (and more) will behave in the future, we really cannot say which is the right amount. It is difficult to ascertain. However, there are two things that need to be kept in mind if you intend to follow the F.I.R.E. strategy.

Firstly, do not forget to live life like a normal person in the present while you are planning to retire early and live a good life in the future. This means if it is not viable to retire early, do not beat yourself in the process to retire early by living an austere life. Secondly, in the journey to become financially independent early on, many individuals follow an equity heavy strategy. This can backfire in times of crisis (or Black Swan events). Equity can take a deep hit when a crisis like the global financial crisis of 2008 or the COVID-19 crisis of 2020 hit the markets. At such times, the F.I.R.E. targets start to seem unviable and you may end up making wrong decisions by taking unsavoury risks. (Someone who sees 30 to 60 percent of their savings erodes in a matter of weeks, typically, is not in their right minds.) Perhaps a factor of safety must be in mind if you are aiming for F.I.R.E.

Two Expectancies

Whether it is F.I.R.E. you are aiming at or retirement as it comes, you are basically estimating two quantities.

1. Life Expectancy: How long you and your partner are likely to live
2. Wealth Expectancy: How long will the money you accumulated or invested will last

So, simply put, when your wealth expectancy is greater than life expectancy, you are financially sorted and can retire from working for money. In a formula:

Retirement Viability = f (Wealth Expectancy > Life Expectancy)

However, it is practically impossible to determine your life expectancy even with the best genetic inputs, lifestyle parameters, and data science. No one till date can predict how long you will live (even astrologers fail here miserably), neither can the lifestyle you will have after 20 years be predicted. You could stay healthy till the end of your days or fall sick and need special care for a long time. No one knows. The uncertainty around retirement can cause anxiety. Certainly, there must be something we can do? Let us understand the other view.

The Other View

Given the importance of retirement and the anxiety around it, there is a lot of research around it. Of late, the research has gone into not solving the problem, but understanding it. Some of the finds are noteworthy. The first is the effect of retirement on health. In a research paper titled *The Effects of Retirement on Physical and Mental Health Outcomes,* by Dhaval Dave, Inas Rashad, *and* Jasmina Spasojevic, the authors note that,

> *"Results indicate that complete retirement leads to a 5-16 percent increase in difficulties associated with mobility and daily activities, a 5-6 percent increase in illness conditions, and 6-9 percent decline in mental health, over an average post-retirement period of six years."*

In short, they note that physical and mental health head south after retirement. They further note that these effects are more if the retirement is involuntary.

Fortunately, these effects get mitigated if the individual is married, has social support, continues to engage in physical activity, or continues to work part-time post-retirement. Further, early retirement leads to strain on the social support and medical system as well. This means that the promises that were made to working individuals in their youth about retirement will fall short of fulfilment, leaving the individuals on their own. This makes us understand that while retirement is a systematic event, it is no longer relevant in the current context especially when individuals live many years post-retirement as well.

So there is a good case to perhaps not retire completely. In their book *Ikigai: The Japanese Secret to a Long and Happy Life*, authors Hector Garcia and Francesc Miralles delve into the lives of super-centenarians - people who live 100 years and longer. They discover that not only are diet, moderate exercise, and community responsible for giving a long happy life, but also the presence of daily working stress and purpose. This means that human beings were designed to live long and well, provided they were productively and meaningfully engaged. Understanding this fact, makes us question the concept of retirement all together!

The Retirement Equilibrium Strategy

This book has been written around the human and financial perspectives of money. Applying this concept to retirement gives us an alternative approach. Consider retirements in two parts:

1. Human Retirement
2. Financial Retirement

For human retirement, the key component is time. Instead of considering retirement as the end of your working career and the beginning of your "no-work life," let retirement be a phase change in the way you allocate time in your day. From that perspective, retirement is a change in the equilibrium of allocating time between working time and personal time. Before retirement, you may be working 8 to 10 hours per day for 5 to 6 days a week. Post-retirement, you can choose to change this equilibrium. Let's understand this with the help of Table 14 below:

Table 14: Retirement Equilibrium Strategy

	Pre-Retirement Schedule	Post-Retirement Schedule
Working Hours vs. **Personal Hours** (Per Day)	8-10 hours vs. 4-6 hours	4-6 hours vs. 8-10 hours
Working Days vs. **Rest Days** (Per Week)	5-6 days vs. 1-2 days	1-3 days vs. 4-6 days

Retirement, from the human perspective, is therefore just a shift of equilibrium in how you divide the 24 hours and 7 days of a week. You are retired when you spend more personal time in the day and more personal days in the week than working hours and days. The retirement formula then becomes:

$$\textit{Human Retirement} = f(\textit{Personal Time} > \textit{Working Time})$$

For a salaried person who is retired involuntarily, this phase change can be on the retirement day (Systematic Retirement), whereas for a professional or a businessperson this phase change can be continuous. Retirement is thus a personal choice. If you have found your Ikigai, you may choose to keep working till the last day of your life! Personally speaking, both of us (the authors) would like to pass away working on our desks with loads of on-going projects.

The shift of equilibrium can also be applied to financial perspective. Whereas time is a human factor, income is a financial factor. The objective of your investing should be transiting your income from active to passive over the years. Ideally, this should happen somewhere in your 40s to the time you systematically retire. In short, financial retirement is when you earn more from your investments than from your active income. Summing up it in a formula:

$$Financial\ Retirement = f(Passive\ Income > Active\ Income)$$

Your retirement objective thus should be to build passive income and never stop working (hopefully pursuing your Ikigai). In today's economy, systematic retirement (or coming to a hard stop at work) is a myth which no longer serves us.

Retirement is all about choice, financially you should have the option to do as you please, the freedom to follow your passion, and be able to pursue your dream without bothering about where the butter for the bread is going to come from. For us, retirement is all about choice, to do as we please.

Chapter 27

How to Handle Extremes

The Cash-out

Before Sumit started to work as a voice-over artist, he was working in IT with a start-up. The start-up was building a digital payments platform. This is where he had met his first boss Jayesh, who to date is a mentor and friend. Sumit had worked there for 6 long years but had finally moved out when he wanted to pursue his interest as a voice-over artist. As early employees, Jayesh and Sumit had primarily been compensated by shareholding of the company along with a salary.

Sumit's initial share was almost 10% of the firm's ownership. However, in subsequent rounds of funding, his share had gone down to 5%. Jayesh's was close to 7.5%. The company was then valued at Rupees 250 million. This was 2 years ago. The founders and the VCs had offered a buyout for Sumit and Jayesh's shares, but they told them that they believed in the company's future and had passed the offer. They expected the valuation to go much higher. The valuation made Sumit feel the warmth and comfort of having a nest egg, but he had not seen the cash as yet. So it was always at the back of his mind.

On a Wednesday morning, at 7 am, Jayesh called Sumit. Sumit was a bit surprised to see Jayesh's call this early in the morning. The first thought that raced in Sumit's mind was that it could be an emergency. He quickly answered. Jayesh was screaming "Woooooooo!" at the top of his voice. Sumit was dumbfounded. He kept silent and let Jayesh stop screaming.

A moment later, Jayesh got himself together and said, "Bro the day we were waiting for has come. We are rich!" Sumit did not get the context and asked for an explanation. Jayesh quickly explained, "Fifteen minutes ago, I got a call from our dear previous boss, Nikhil, that the company has received another round of funding. The valuation now stands at Rupees 1 Billion!" Sumit gasped, he realized that as per their initial agreement, the mandatory buy out clause had triggered for both him and Jayesh. He calculated he would be paid out Rupees 50 Million. He was a crorepati now.

Human Extremes

Extremes happen to all of us sometime in our lives. These extremes can be positive or negative. The one thing common about extremes, whether positive or negative, is that they impact us financially. For each extreme or outlier event in our lives, we end up gaining or losing money. These extremes are rare and may happen to us only once in our lifetimes. Typically, we are never prepared for such extremes because there is no reference guide available. There is the advice of experienced elders, but we seldom pay heed to it. Only after the fact do we know that we had to take care of such an aspect as well.

Sumit hitting a Rupees 50 Million payout is a positive extreme. So are getting an unexpected sum, or assets in inheritance, or selling a successful business, or cashing stock options at a huge multiple, or unexpected returns on forgotten investments, or discovery of natural resources on land you own, or even hitting the jackpot of a lottery. These positive extremes are called windfall.

There can be many sources of a windfall. However, the two things common to all these reasons are:

1. It is sudden and unexpected.
2. It has a huge financial gain and changes the current financial status.

Most people who receive a windfall are not prepared to handle it. Often, unprepared receivers can end up losing or squandering much of their gains and regret it later. In fact, according to a non-profit organisation, The National Endowment for Financial Education in the United States, studies show that 70% of lottery winners go bust within 5 years. This means there is a huge probability that it can happen to more people than not. Even for the 30% of people who do not go bust, not everyone is able to keep or grow all of the winnings. A very small percentage is actually able to internalize the gains. The only ones who are able to internalize the gains are the ones who are prepared.

So how should you handle a windfall? There is no straight answer. We can give you a short plan, but the details are best handled by a financial advisor. Let us take Sumit's case to understand this.

Internalizing a Windfall

Sumit is set to receive INR 50 million. The first thing that will happen even before he can touch the money is taxes. Sumit will have to pay about 10% of the earnings as long term capital gains after indexation, deductions, and adjustments. The government always gets paid, whosoever it may be. This is a fact. So Sumit will be left with around INR 45 million.

To be able to internalize it, he should keep 20% of the winnings for future use. This means he needs to pay his future self. Accordingly, INR 10 million should go into solid low-risk investments. Say a basic mixture of debt and equity yielding 10% per annum post-tax on an average will give him INR 50 million again in about 17 years. So his long term goals are settled. Now he is left with INR 35 million.

Next, he should use another 5% to enjoy and meet his "enjoy life" goal. It is always better to "*stop and smell the roses*" along the way rather than continue arduously on the life journey without an enjoyable moment! It is prudent to make your loved ones and yourself happy so you can keep a balanced head.

Sumit can use INR 2.5 million for whatever he wants. He can buy a car, or go on vacations every year for the next 5 years. In fact, by spending money on himself and his family he can blow out any splurge urges. This will set him up for internalizing the rest of the money. Now he is left with INR 32.5 million still!

A 2008 study by Harvard Business School professor Michael Norton and his colleagues showed that giving away money increases our happiness more than consuming it by ourselves. This was a practice followed by the ancient Babylonians called the Tithing Law and even finds mention in the Sikh scriptures as *"Dassawan"*. Sumit can choose to share some part of his money with his loved ones or give to charity. By sharing, Sumit makes more people happy around him or in society. Happiness comes back manifold. However, this is a personal choice. Say Sumit gives away 5% of his winnings, he is now left with INR 30 million.

What next? Sumit has a house loan and some credit card debts too. Sumit should offload his debt. This is a tough task to do, especially when flawed logic float in the society, which say:

> *"You can pay off the debt with your salary,*
> *invest the money instead."*

This statement is nothing short of a disaster. We often meet individuals who have confidence that they can pay off the debt from their future earnings and the money they have now should be invested.

In Chapter 24, "Reading the Fine Print", we discussed that debt makes you leveraged and susceptible to amplified financial shocks. Unless you have secured a sure-shot source of income which provides 5% more returns than the cost of debt, you should end all debt immediately with any windfall gains. There is no sure-shot source of income discovered so far which can give 5% more than the cost of debt. Debt is never cheap. It carries a higher interest rate than any sure-shot compound interest you can earn. This is how banks function, by giving you a sure-shot interest rate on your deposits and earning more on what they lend.

Let's say Sumit is left with INR 18 million after paying debt on his home loan and credit card bills. What should he do with this? He should immediately put this money into government cash. This means he puts his money in an overnight fund which invests money in government cash instruments. This is essential since he will not have the money in his bank and it will help him keep his head straight and avoid any temptations. Sumit should now hire a financial advisor and figure out his priorities again. Priorities change when long term liabilities are retired and long term goals are met. In Sumit's case, his funding capacity has also changed because his EMI is no longer going to be there. He has freed up cash income which he can invest to meet any other goals. Since Sumit is no longer leveraged with debt, his risk profile will change too. This means Sumit needs to reconfigure his priorities and actions using the 5/25 rule (discussed in Chapter 22).

Every individual and family setup has different needs. In Sumit's case, both he and his wife are soft skill professionals. Sumit is a freelancer and may have income augmentation needs (having a passive regular cash flow supplementing the fluctuating income he earns as a freelancer). He can internalize the balance of his winnings by setting up an income portfolio. For this too he should take the advice of a financial advisor.

The Opposite Extreme

Unexpected things happen on the negative side of the spectrum too. Even if you are careful about the risks you know about, there are always some events which can happen to you and are unknown to you as well. These are called catastrophes. Catastrophes like critical illnesses to self or family members, accidents (personal and material), relationship disagreements like divorces, inheritance disputes, the downfall of a business, or loss of a job and the rise of a legal liability happen to many people. If you live a normal life, the opposite extreme will get to you or those around you at some point in time.

Catastrophic personal events should not scare you, but you should be resilient enough to get back on your feet. While you cannot prepare for everything, you can have a plan for the unexpected. Here are the first few things you can prepare for known exigent circumstances.

1. Income replacement: This means in case of any exigency you should be able to get some income for the time you cannot generate any income or for the dependents in your family. The tool to do this is insurance. Life, medical, home, fire, personal accident, and all sorts of insurances can be used depending on the circumstances of the individual.

2. Contingency fund: You should have a nest egg for rainy days. A contingency fund is a buffer for your immediate needs if the income gets disturbed. Typically, you should have a contingency fund worth 6 to 12 months of your consumables expenses (not income).

3. Diversify income sources: While all is well and the sun is shining, make hay. A good job or business is your active income. However, you should seriously consider and work towards passive sources of income. If you have some talents, you can set them up to earn royalties or license a subscription. Alternately, you can invest and build passive financial income from fixed income instruments and rental income from property.

Finally, have a catastrophic liquidation plan. You can do some of the following in case of an exigent situation.

1. Cut on lifestyle expenses immediately. This will lower your expenses. Every household knows at the back of their heads what excesses they splurge on. Decide what is essential and what is luxury. You can always get back to luxury later in better circumstances. (Easier said than done though).

2. If more cash is required, then first liquidate assets which act as a store of value or are to be consumed. This means if you need a substantial

amount of money, sell the gold. Assets like gold jewellery, precious stones, Veblen goods like watches, expensive cars, collectables, art, antiques are of no use going forward. You are less likely to wear your watches and jewellery if you are facing financial hardships. This also requires overcoming strong emotional barriers. In India, there is a special affinity to gold jewellery and it is considered a matter of pride not to liquidate it even in exigent times. This is a personal choice and up to individuals and family to take it up. You can build up these assets again, in better times.

3. Finally, even if more cash is required, liquidate your financial assets. This means you should consider selling your portfolio of assets like mutual funds, stocks, bonds, etc. the last. Of these, sell the ones which are most speculative in nature (and are selling at good valuations as well.) This will require careful consideration to differentiate between the two and can be challenging in a complex portfolio. A financial advisor can help. You should consider selling equity the last because it will help you get up back again.

Even though we have listed possible steps for a catastrophic liquidation plan here, they will be seldom followed. In fact, individuals and families follow the reverse order. They liquidate equities and bonds first, then gold and other such assets, and finally only then cut down their lifestyle. It is an emotionally challenging situation where thinking straight can be tough. However, having thought of a plan beforehand can be helpful just like Captain Suraj Rathi when he had to manage engine failure.

Financial Extremes - Black Swans

Nassim Nicholas Taleb first defined the term Black Swan in 2008, in his book titled *Black Swan*. Today, the word is very commonly used by the financial media and finance professionals. A Black Swan has three characteristics:

1. It comes by surprise. Nobody can ever predict it or know that it could happen.
2. It has a very deep, irreversible, and widespread (negative) impact on almost everyone.
3. Post the event, people come up with theories that it was bound to happen and that it was in front of their eyes.

Black Swan events happen more often than not in today's world. Given their unpredictable nature, Black Swan events can only be prepared for with robust systems (though Taleb says it should be *Antifragile* systems). This means one needs to have a plan and try to stick to it. So what should you do if there is a Black Swan event like the global financial crisis of 2008, or the demonetization in India in 2016, or the COVID-19 crisis in 2020? Use the following plan:

1. Recognize that it is happening with everyone. Unlike a human extreme, which will make you relatively less wealthy than others, a financial extreme makes everyone poor in proportion to their wealth.
2. Do not act with urgency instinct. The urgency instinct is the need to do something about the situation. As described by Hans Rosling in the book *Factfulness*, urgency instinct, when triggered, shuts down our analysis capability. We just want to do something when markets are falling. The only thing you should do when the markets are falling is to do nothing! If your portfolio is well planned then you can rest assured that "*this too shall pass.*" Remember:

> "*The time to be defensive is not during a crisis but before a crisis.*"

3. Have a plan to profit from disaster. If you are an experienced investor or your money is managed by one, then you will have a plan of actions for Black Swan events. How you react to this event will decide whether you come up with a winner or loser. In order to profit from such an event, have a Black Swan fund. A Black Swan fund, like a contingency

fund, is primarily made up of cash and equivalents. It is to be used to purchase high quality, well-diversified portfolios only in both debt and equity. Ace investors like Howard Marks, Ray Dalio, and Warren Buffet sit on billions of dollars of cash, waiting to be deployed in such times. They call such a situation "a once in a lifetime sale." The trick is to pick good quality in bad times in debt and equity. Once deployed, you may have to sit on the fund for 2-5 years for the value to unlock and realize the gains.

4. Do not stop the SIP. Markets recover very fast. Very few individuals or algorithms can recognize the reversals and time them. It is better to average down than to time the bottom (in case of markets, not stocks!). A SIP is essentially a good averaging tool (for new capital to be deployed). If you have a pile of cash, then deploy it and wait. Do not SIP the Black Swan fund over many months.

Positive financial extremes which make everyone rich suddenly are unheard of. There is no point in everyone getting rich at the same time. Wealth is relative. If everyone's financial situation improves, it is not getting rich, it is social progress.

Chapter 28

Keeping Wealth

Sameer and Sumit are tennis fans. When they were growing up, they played tennis and followed stars like Andre Agassi, Pete Sampras, Boris Becker, Martina Navratilova, Steffi Graf, and to date still follow Roger Federer, Rafael Nadal, Serena Willams, and Novak Djokovic. Successful tennis players make huge amounts of money during their careers. Their fortunes run into millions which come not only from the match fees and tournament winnings, but also from brand endorsements, business partnerships, and other investments. However, not everyone who earns money remains perpetually wealthy. This is because earning wealth requires hard work and luck, but keeping wealth also requires hard work and planning. Having lots of money doesn't make you good at managing it. Let's understand this with a story of success and failure each.

Boom Boom

Boris Becker won his first Wimbledon title at age 17. He was the youngest unseeded player to do so. Over his career from 1984 to 1999, he won 6 grand slam titles, an Olympic gold in men's double, 5-year end championships, and 13 masters series titles. Becker was known as "Boom Boom" because of his ferocious serve. The making of Borris Becker, the grand slam master, contains playing non-stop from the age of 7; millions of Deutsche Mark spent on training, and countless daily hours put in by multiple coaches over his career. Even after his retirement from professional playing in 1999, Becker still made his mark on tennis. As coach of Djokovic, Becker oversaw him win 6 major titles over three years. He also headed the men's tennis for the German Tennis Foundation.

At the height of his career, Becker had amassed US$ 63 million in prize money and sponsorships. On top of it, he was a superb poker player and is known to have appeared in the European Poker Tour and World Poker Tour. Becker won around US$ 100,000 over his poker career. He appeared in TV shows, published his autobiography, launched an online media platform featuring clips from his career. He owned his personal line of tennis racquets and clothing as well. If there was fame and heights in the career of Borris Becker, it was purely due to hard work and a good amount of luck.

Yet in 2017, Boris Becker filed for bankruptcy and was declared bankrupt by the Bankruptcy and Companies Court in the UK. His attorney described him as, "… *not a sophisticated individual when it comes to finances.*" He was indebted to a bank for US$ 14 million, and to his former business advisor for US$ 41 million. A bitter and long divorce with his first wife Feltus cost him US$ 25 million. His second wife Lilly divorced him because of financial disarray. Further, a sports website, an organic food business, and a tower planned to be named after him in Dubai, all failed for him. In 2012, he fell behind in his debts owed to the contractors for work on his luxury villa. To cover these debts, his 62 acre complex, with a guesthouse, pool, tennis and basketball courts, and an orange grove, was repossessed and disposed of. In 2019, his trophies, memorabilia and collectables were auctioned off for his bankruptcy. He is currently going to be considered bankrupt till October 2031.

Pistol Pete

Pete Sampras started playing tennis against a wall at age 3. He played professional tennis from 1988 till 2002. However, he was not a first-time shocker. He had to work his way up the rankings through wins and losses. By his second pro year, he only managed to move from number 97 to number 81 in the pro rankings. Even by 1992, he kept reaching quarter-finals of major titles and kept losing. So Sampras changed tactics and worked harder. In 1993, he became the world no. 1, but it was controversial because there was no major title victory attained recently. Later that year, however, he won his first Wimbledon title and thereafter he was unstoppable. By the end of his career, he had won 7 Wimbledon titles and 14 Grand Slam titles in total. He was ranked world no. 1 for a total of 286 weeks, a record only broken by Roger Federer in a different era.

Pete Sampras was precise in what he did. His serve earned him the name "Pistol Pete" because of the precision and power he put behind it each time. He only got there through practice, persistence, and most importantly through focus. Sampras is said to have earned a career winning north of US$ 43 million. However, his estimated worth is US$ 168 million. Sampras made the extra figures not only from brand endorsements but also through investments. One such area is real estate. In 2009, he bought a California home worth $US 5.9 million and modified it. Later, he sold it off for US$ 7.25 million. Sampras is known to have build up from scratch and traded many California mansions. Sampras not only added features to the house but also added his brand. Sampras was not a real estate professional to start with, but learnt the ropes through many deals in real estate. He specifically stuck to high-end residential real estate and traded slowly.

Both Borris Becker and Pete Sampras were contemporaries. Both were legends of their times and earned huge sums of money through hard work and persistence. Both were lucky enough to get great endorsements and earn even more. Most of these endorsements were of similar types of brands and sports-related goods. While Borris Becker earned US$ 63 million over his career, Pete Sampras earned US$ 43 million. Yet today, one is bankrupt and the other is many times more his sports earnings' net worth.

Getting Rich vs Staying Rich

Both men became rich by playing professional tennis. However, staying rich and creating wealth out of those riches is another ball game. Simply put, it is a constant struggle. This ballgame was something that Pete Sampras played after his tennis career and Boris Becker did not. Perhaps their blueprint about wealth was what made all the difference.

Wealth is not about making a huge corpus and enjoying it, as Borris Becker did. It is more about creating a corpus and working hard to keep it growing and generating income out of it, perpetually. This means there has to be the preservation of wealth as well, not just growth and enjoyment. Let us understand these things.

Preserving Wealth

Wealth can be hard-earned (as in the case of both Becker and Sampras) or it can come from a stroke of luck as in the case of Sumit (in Chapter 27), where his hard work paid off disproportionately (hard work was done nonetheless). Wealth can even come from the role of chance as in the case of an unexpected inheritance. In any case, the first objective is to preserve wealth. Here are a few things to do to achieve that.

1. Reduce your exposure to randomness. Markets are random in nature. Randomness works in your favour when you have more to gain than to lose. For a wealthy person, this is inverse. By participating in randomness, they might make even more money, but they may also lose a lot of it. Consequently, a wealthy person preserves their wealth by putting a bulk of their money in low-risk compounding instruments i.e., accumulation without randomness. If your wealth is liquid, you could do this by investing in government bonds, or participate in arbitrage through mutual funds or a long-short alternative investment fund, or even park cash in TREPS for a short term. There are many large ticket options like a commercial (rent generating) real estate. However, those should be tread carefully. In short, if you are wealthy,

you need not take macho risks. There is nothing sexy about losing money.

2. Insist on a margin of safety. You may have come this far by being brave and taking aggressive risks, but it no longer makes sense to continue doing so. Preserving wealth requires that you act proactively. Any asset which you own, which is more than 10% of your net worth, needs to be insured. If you own prime real estate, get its appropriate insurances. If you own a business, get it insured. If you have a large portfolio of stocks, hedge it from time to time. Insurance might mean a recurring cost, but it's worth it. You can even insure your reputation because getting discredited could cost a lot. A margin of safety always seems redundant, but when it insulates you from harm, it seems like a little cost with great benefit.

3. Stay within your circle of competence. You got wealthy, great! However, it pays to remember that you are not good at everything. In Chapter 18, we saw that Rahul had great success in business and stocks markets. Yet when he ventured out of his circle of competence and invested in venture capital all by himself, he suffered a loss. In real life, this is what happened to Borris Becker. He invested in ventures he had no understanding of, let alone having any expertise on. On top of it, he made the same mistake again and again by investing in one risky venture after another. He thought that investing was enough. However, being able to manage and turn those ventures into profit is not the same as playing tennis. (That is why you need a general partner and a fund manager for investing in venture capital.) Being successful in one field does not give anyone the license to succeed in all other fields. Stay in your field of work. Pete Sampras understood high end residential real estate and did not stray from this asset class.

4. Diversify, wisely! You need not be invested in one field, one market, or even one country. Spread your money in parts around the globe. Do not go shopping for the next big thing. There are enough conservative things to diversify in, all through the globe. The same working and

time tested systems work all through the globe. It is wise to consult multiple advisors on different parts of the portfolio. Always diversify the advice you receive. A great way to ensure this diversity of advice is to form a *family office* to handle a windfall or a fortune.

Growing Wealth

After you set up yourself to preserve your wealth, your next step is to grow it. If you do not give full-time effort to growing your wealth, you will not stay wealthy. The key is to understand that wealth is relative, it is on the move. Rich people do not always sail in yachts, they work hard to discover deals and make more money out of them. So here is a brief guideline.

1. Focus on the T. We discussed compounding in Chapter 6. Compounding has three components to it. The initial principal, the rate of return, and time. For an equal increase in each of these factors, time pays the most. The longer the time, the more is the effect of compounding. Growing wealth is about keeping it long enough for it to grow even more. Most people focus on growing faster (i.e. the rate of return). However, it is all about growing it longer. In Pete Sampras's case, he made multiple deals in real estate and grew his money manifold before he started to use it for his enjoyment. Delayed gratification is a principle which works at every stage and is based on the T.

2. Look for a sustainable advantage. Many things work and give profits. However, not many things give profits (or generate returns) consistently. This is why real estate is one of the most favourite asset classes of the wealthy. Not only does it grow in value, but also it gives out income in the form of rent. This is common knowledge to everyone and many people try to replicate this by investing in rent yielding real estate. Yet not everyone who buys a piece of real estate becomes even richer. The difference lies in the quality of the real estate. Good quality real estate which pays rent for very long periods and still manages to grow

decently comes at a price. This is the difference. Duplication should not be done at the scaled-down version. It simply is not sustainable.

3. Use market cycles. You should not time the markets: true. However, you should take cognisance of market cycles. To quote Nasim Nicholas Taleb from his book *Antifragile*, "*People become rich by not going bust (particularly when others do)*." The key ability to grow wealth is to not get poor when everyone else is getting poor. This means knowing when to sell, booking profits, and taking a back seat. Timing exits is perhaps the most difficult job, not because it is intellectually challenging, but also because it is emotionally challenging. Market wisdom says it is better to make less money than to lose money. So there will be times when you exit and are out of the market, and the market keeps on going higher. It will be tough at those moments to stand against the euphoria of the crowd and seem like a fool. Market entries, however, are easier emotionally, you just have to buy into the negative sentiment. Market cycles are a key tool to grow your wealth. However, you will need the assistance of many experts (human, algos, and machine) to know when to execute the moves.

4. Take only extreme volatility (in small bites). More risk means more reward. This is generally true. However, if you find something which has less risk and very high rewards, use the cross-boxed framework and be suspicious. Wealthy people can take extreme risks and get very highly favourable outcomes, provided they take these risks in small bites and have a calculated downside. Typically, such risks will have half or double outcome, with more probability of double than half. Such opportunities come with extreme volatility. Another concept to understand here is that high returns not only come with high volatility but also have a limit to size. This means a high yielding strategy will have a limit to the amount of money that can be deployed in it. So once the limit is reached, and you have even more funds to deploy, diversify. Find many opportunities to take risk rather than one.

The Barbell Strategy

For preserving wealth we told you to decrease your exposure to randomness, and for growing wealth, we told you to take on extreme volatility. These are contradictory because extreme volatility comes with randomness. However, these two things go hand in hand. It is only a matter of proportion. The result is a barbell strategy. In a barbell strategy portfolio, an investor only invests in the extremes of risk. This means the exposure of their money is with the safest type of strategies or to the riskiest type of strategies. The middle or balanced risk is avoided altogether.

To understand this, follow the example below.

Consider that you want equity-like returns in your portfolio in the long run. Equity typically has a real return of around 5% (This means if the index returns 12% and the inflation is 6.66%, the real return after discounting inflation would be 5% - refer Chapter 6; If inflation goes up, the return on equity goes up and vice versa).

You can achieve this return in another way too. If you put 60% of your money in risk-free cash at 3.5%, and 40% of your money in various instruments which yield around 24.75%, then you can get the same rate of growth as 12% in equity. However, your volatility is much lower. This is because the cash at 3.5% has near 0% volatility. An instrument which yields 2 times the return as the index will not necessarily have 2 times the volatility.

However, this strategy will have other constraints. Certain high yielding instruments will have a large ticket size and will not be accessible to individuals with smaller portfolios. So for all practical purposes, the barbell strategy changes as wealth level changes. As wealth level increases, even higher risk strategies open up. To balance the volatility, even lower risk strategies need to be added. This means that while the barbell of a young new investor may contain debt and large cap equity, the barbell of a multi-generational wealthy family may contain early-stage venture equity and overnight funds (exposed to TREPS). Figure 10 shows how volatility is balanced out for riskier strategies taken up by individuals and families with high wealth levels.

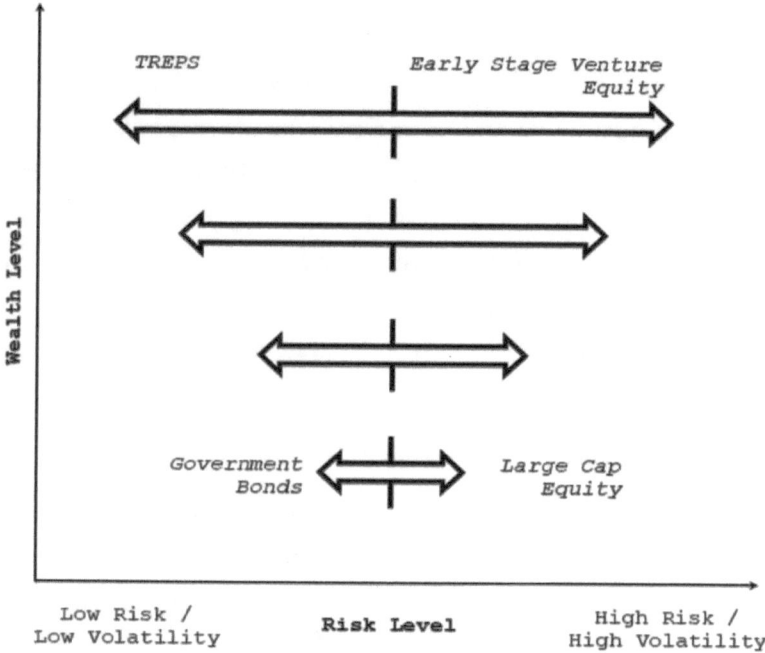

Figure 10: Barbell Strategy with Wealth Levels

We also recommend that such strategies be only implemented after consulting specific professionals. There are many more strategies that are employed by the wealthy to preserve and grow wealth. They are beyond the scope of this book.

Enjoying Wealth

Keeping and growing wealth is not the final objective of wealth. Enjoying it and living a better life is. While there is a whole list of things you can do to enjoy wealth, we will only discuss 4 (to keep it short and simple).

1. Don't do it all in one go. If you have worked hard for making wealth, you must spend some of it to enjoy life. However, this does not have to be done in one go. Becker did it in one go. He made too many purchases in a short time. He inflated his lifestyle in a boom and was then unable to manage its expenses. Living like a rich person takes time. You have to understand what something is worth before

you spend on it. For example, you should not buy a new car because you can. You should buy one because you need to. This is superbly followed by Warren Buffet (as we discussed in Chapter 3). He only buys a new car when the previous one gets old. There too he sticks to his choice and doesn't unnecessarily upgrade his preferences. Upgrades should be done one at a time. That is how you enjoy your wealth over a longer period. Many newly minted rich people also increase the value of their consumption. They do this by spending more money on the same things. Consuming things you do not really like, but doing it anyway because they cost more, is vain. It is like buying Swiss dark chocolate when you are a fan of the Indian version, just because you can. Keep your consumption stable and change it slowly.

2. Share it the right way. The wealthy like to give back to society. They do this by contributing to a cause or starting a charity of their own, or in any other way. This is a personal choice and many times very close to the heart of a wealthy person or family. Sharing wealth for a cause is a noble thing to do. However, it should be done in the right way. The right way is making it sustainable.

   Just giving money is not enough. You must set up a source for the perpetual funding of the cause like a trust or an endowment fund. This means setting up an institution which is run like a business. The institution should be able to fund itself after being set up with your initial contribution. This will require your time as well. An example of this is Tata Trust. There is more satisfaction in giving time and involvement than just giving money.

3. Make your relationships better. Money is a magnifier. It magnifies whatever there is. If there is a bad relationship, wealth will magnify it and make it even more troublesome. Keeping good and clean relationships takes a lot of effort. Ideally, this should be done before you become rich. The wealthy spend a lot of time and effort to maintain good relationships. This is because wealth can be lost because of poor relationships. We have come across numerous cases

where a fallout between heirs caused the family fortune to wither away. The same is true for romantic and marital relationships. Becker's first divorce was because of his own infidelity and cost him a lot. His second divorce was because of financial disarray. Relationships can also wither as wealth withers. Sampras, on the other hand, kept a stable and sporting partnership with his wife Bridget Wilson since 2000. Some relationships come with exposures because of the laws of the land. These too need to be taken care of. Typically, the wealthy will form structures to protect from these exposures. The best solution is to work on your relationships and make them better so they can withstand the rise and fall of fortunes. Nevertheless, some relations will still go sour. Bad luck.

4. Pass it on. Have a legacy mindset. If you have earned wealth and have further generations then plan to pass it on by leaving a legacy. The wealthy create systems in the form of wealth management entities. Today there are many such entities available. These can be a full-time distributor whose earnings are directly linked to your corpus, an investment advisor who is mandated to act as a fiduciary, a single or multi-family office which goes beyond just wealth management. The options are available to everyone as per the size and complexity of their wealth and can be upgraded as wealth grows.

In the next chapter of this book, we want to discuss how to choose these options.

Chapter 29

Invest In and With An Advisor

At a student interaction, Warren Buffett, the legendary investor, was asked what surprises him the most. He replied pointing to Bill Gates who was standing next to him and said,

"People look at Bill Gates and think they can't do what he did. They look at me and think they can do what I did."

For some reason, everyone believes they can manage their money proficiently even though history has a completely different story which says that while investment returns have been spectacular, investors have returned empty-handed or have abysmally little to talk about. This is evident in that while the SENSEX has grown from 100 in the year 1979 to 49000 today, very few investors have been able to capture these returns. This is perhaps because the art of money management is mistaken as a science.

The paradox of art or science is true for any skilled profession. Doctors, lawyers, artisans of any sort, all take some formal training at some point in time. After that, they work for a few years as apprentices and only then do they get down to their own practice. They learn the science and then practice it as an art. The same is true for investing. However, people do not even learn the science of investing. They think that watching a TV channel and reading articles/reports on the internet is enough to make them an expert.

So if you consult a doctor or a lawyer for your specific needs, does an advisor too really help in managing money? What is the exact role an advisor plays? These are the questions that plague an investor in the era of direct plans, discount brokerages, and one-size fit all robo-advisories, all of which can be accessed with a smartphone.

The Cost of an Advisor

There are plenty of reasons for DIY investing (discussed in Chapter 21) and going without an advisor or going direct, not adopting the DIFM (Do It For Me). However, studies have shown that investors generally get an inferior return when they go direct. This is mainly because their investment journey is shorter. With no one to guide or handhold, investors react to the market volatility, try to time the market, and give unfounded allocations of assets in their portfolios, thereby getting sub-optimal returns.

Investors often do not link their investments to goals. Goal linked or mapped investments are more disciplined and help the investor prevail in choppy markets. Advisors help investors map goals and also keep investors focused on them so that they do not quit the market in choppy times.

Vanguard, one of the world's largest investment companies, has been examining this question for more than 15 years. Based on their research, Vanguard has concluded that:

> *"Yes, there is a quantifiable increase in return from working with a financial advisor."*

Vanguard calls this advantage the advisor's alpha. When certain best practices are followed, the result can be an alpha in the range of 3 percent per year.

Russell Investments Canada Ltd.'s "*2019 Value of an Advisor*" study backs this fact. It concluded that the value a trusted advisor adds to an investor's portfolio (apart from investment gains) is 2.79 percent in the preceding year, which "*materially exceeds the 1 per cent fee advisors typically charge for their services.*" This figure is about 4.6 percent in the U.S. and 4.4 percent in Australia. Hence, the cost of an advisor is taken care of by the advisor's alpha.

Managing the Human Perspective

Data also indicates that financial advisors can provide the most valuable assistance during periods of high market volatility when investors are most likely to react with their emotions instead of logic. A study by Morningstar shows that investors often receive far lower returns than the very funds they invest in. The reason: "Investors run to funds after they have done well and ditch other funds right before they take off." In other words, they sell low and buy high. An advisor can prevent such counterproductive behaviour. But the single biggest way a financial advisor can add value—up to 1.5 percent per year of increased annual returns—is through behavioural coaching.

Research in behavioural finance shows that cognitive biases and other behavioural obstacles often inhibit investors from making sound financial decisions, especially when their emotions are running high. Advisors help clients in different situations like a market crash, avoiding the mania of herd investing, helping overcome choice paralysis, and other behavioural biases. Vanguard's study shows that advisors can add 150 bps (1.5 percent) additional returns through behavioural coaching alone.

The great Sachin Tendulkar had a guru, Nadal and Federer even after winning close to 10+ Grand Slams still needed the guidance of a coach. Amitabh Bachchan also needs a director to tell him what to do in a movie. We all attend seminars and classes to keep ourselves updated despite the information available on the net. For excellence in any field, we need a "*guru*".

The coach or advisor tells us the best possible way to go about it, to adopt the right technique, make course corrections when required, to ensure that you don't injure yourself, to optimize the available resources, to overcome the mandatory volatility and failures we will encounter on the way, for hand-holding during difficult times, and to help us achieve that little extra on our way to the goal post.

Investment is not all about quantitative techniques and numbers. We are all human and we react to different situations differently. The most common biases in human behaviour are the ones related to our money and investment habits. When it comes to money and investing, we're not always as rational as we think we are. Most economic theory is based on the belief that individuals behave in a rational manner and that all existing information is embedded in the investment process. However, human emotions influence investors in their decision-making process and information asymmetries exist.

Every good poker player knows, scared money doesn't make money. Similarly, the best financial advisors are able to keep their clients' fears and emotions in check by providing steady, fact-based advice and reassurance when the markets get wobbly or crazy. This is the single largest benefit of working with a financial advisor.

There are several other ways in which a financial advisor can add value to your investment efforts. Each of these services can incrementally boost an investor's returns. Among the benefits are guidance on financial budgeting, quantifying goals, risk tolerance levels, developing an overall investment strategy, asset allocation, minimizing taxes, portfolio re-balancing, how to structure/time withdrawals from your corpus, and, above all, to help you overcome volatility in the investment journey.

Don't Cheat Yourself

Another thing to note is that as an investor, you do not end up cheating yourself. Say you go to a doctor and you have an upset stomach. The doctor will prescribe some medicines and probably ask you to abstain from food for a day. However, if you forget to mention to the doctor that you are slightly diabetic, you are likely to end up in more trouble because your blood sugar levels may get upset if you do not eat. A doctor simply needs to have a holistic view of your health status (even if she is not the one you are consulting for your diabetes management). By not disclosing your diabetes condition to the doctor who is curing you for an upset stomach, you are cheating yourself.

The same happens with a financial advisor. If you do not disclose to your advisor what your entire portfolio looks like (probably with the inhibition that they may charge a higher fee) you are likely to set yourself up for a bigger fail. This is because a financial advisor may set your asset allocation and suggest investment strategies according to your wealth level. This is something determined by the portfolio she is aware of. Anything different would need a different solution altogether.

We know of clients who try to replicate the advice given for a smaller portfolio onto a much larger one by themselves. While they do save fees in the short run, they end up losing a lot of money because the asset allocation and investment strategy given by a financial advisor for INR 10,00,000/- is much different for a portfolio of INR 10,00,00,000/-. Such investors end up getting much lower returns if not losing money. This is the worst form of DIY investing. There'd rather be no advisor than an advisor kept in the dark.

Choosing the Right Advisor

Not everyone is suitable to advise everybody. Choosing an advisor is a deliberate choice and should be made with careful consideration. This one decision, if done well, takes care of a lot of other decisions. Here is a list of things you need to consider when choosing an advisor.

1. Size: Every advisor will want to advise the biggest possible client. However, the right advisor will advise the clients whose asset size they can handle. Such advisors will choose to grow by growing their client's assets. An advisor who handles clients with a corpus of Rs. 5 million is very different from the one who handles a corpus of Rs. 50 million or Rs. 500 million. Most advisors will be handling corpus around their average client size, with a few exceptions. Choosing an advisor that

manages a corpus of your starting size will ensure you pay relevant fees and have easy access to investment options relevant to you.

2. Mode: In-person or online is the question most people ask when considering an advisor. Typically, this is governed by convenience and complexity of advisory needs. Busy people feel that a few clicks are more convenient than on phone conversations or meetings in person.

   As a rule of thumb, if you have a financial investment only portfolio, you can choose any mode. However, if you have a portfolio which also contains non-financial investments then you will need in-person advisory. There is also a thought about cost. In-person advisors cost more than online ones. The third factor is emotion. Typically, if you are an emotional person you may need an in-person touch from time to time. Presently, there is a rise in hybrid online/in-person advisory. Typically, operations are managed digitally because of the convenience and the many advantages they offer.

3. Specific needs: Everyone has different needs. A young person may have dependents and an older person may not have a job. In such cases, discovering goals and exploring solutions around them become more important than returns. There are specialist advisors available for such needs. They can be advisors for investments, retirement, insurance, tax, debt, estate planning, and so on. It is important to understand that your advisor may not be an expert in all areas. So seek specialists for complex needs. You can consult multiple advisors, but ensure that they are not of the same domain.

4. Personality: All of us have different outlooks towards life. In the case of financial advice, the objective is to get the job done. At times there can be stark personality differences between the giver and receiver of advice. This difference may come in the way of effectively implementing advice or even formulating advice. Personal compatibility is a must for in-person advisory. An important attribute to look for in your advisor is respect for your goals and empathy towards your risk-taking ability and needs.

What to Expect

A good advisor will nudge you to review your investment strategy regularly. The advisor will not only review how the investments are performing, but also review the performance against goals from time to time. Invariably goals change; the daughter's education plan from a top-notch Indian institution may change to plans to join an Ivy league college abroad, plans for the purchase of a 3BHK in the suburbs may shift to a luxury penthouse downtown. If required, the advisor will take corrective action and do asset rebalancing based on changed requirements. This is important because needs or goals are dynamic and not constant.

A key thing about good advisors is that they do not hesitate to ask the tough questions. A good advisor will also educate you. The intent here is not to make you an expert, but to familiarize you with investment concepts, risks involved, decision making, and increase your general level of sophistication around investing. Such advisors will communicate. This communication will help you understand the happenings in the financial world and for a better view of volatility in the markets.

People believe that a financial advisor is an investment manager, but the larger role of an advisor is that of an "investor" manager. A good financial advisor doesn't only manage an investor's money but also their emotions so as to maximize returns by optimizing the risk-return matrix and controlling the fear and greed. Don't expect your advisor to be like a magic wand which can achieve anything, but like a walking stick, which will give you support, help navigate obstacles, and give you the strength to stand up and move on.

We shall like to end with a simple fact that you always need to remember,

"The best advice may not look the best in the beginning."

Chapter 30

Good Advice Never Changes

"Write to be understood, speak to be heard, and read to grow."

— *Lawrence Clark Powell*

To write about 75 thousand words for this book, we have read more than a few million words each, researching published texts, spent several hours watching videos and audio material, and innumerable hours talking and advising investors. We distilled concepts that we thought were essential and filtered experiences of great investors and *gurus* of the financial world.

Our readathon helped us grow and reach a better understanding of the subject, but so did our disagreements. These disagreements had to be verified and substantiated by research and, in the process, many of our own fundamentals and misconceptions got cleared as well. Most of the situations, stories, and the experiences of Sameer and his associates mentioned in the book have been our own experiences or interactions with investors.

Before writing about *"What my MBA didn't teach me about Money"*, we carried out a small informal survey regarding the role of money in the lives of people. We wanted to know what does it really mean for people to be wealthy. We inquired about their positive and negative experiences with money which come to their mind immediately. We asked them what they would do if they received a sudden windfall and also how much did they think they needed to live the life they always wanted.

We wanted to answer, when it comes to money, do rich people behave differently? Or do they make the same mistakes? What drives financial behaviour? Can children be taught about good financial practices, or do we leave it for them to understand from their own life experiences, because "*we only believe what we see.*"

The role of the human perspective and financial perspective of money became evident from that survey. We also understood that everyone has different money worries. There is neither a single problem nor a single solution related to money. Things also get out of control for many people for reasons beyond their control.

"Money means different things for different people at different times and also holds different value at different times." Chris Rock once said, "If Bill Gates woke up one day with Oprah Winfrey's money, he'd jump out of the window and slit his throat on the way down saying, *I can't even put gas in my plane!*"

Most people have a hard time discussing money and especially their financial struggles. Couples would rather talk about sex or even infidelity than how to handle family finances and money struggles. It's a tough topic. We too don't have all the answers but here are some key takeaways.

Do Not Have Amorphous Financial Goals

Investors have an amorphous financial goal of amassing a large amount of wealth which will last generations. These goals are not specific and quantified and have no timeline. In fact, if you go deeper, you will realise, "Do they really want it or is it just to impress the Jains?"

Most people don't know how they spend their money and the result of a budgeting exercise that we carry out with them is a shock for them. Lack of planning becomes a lack of finances very soon. As Warren Buffet wisely said,

> "An idiot with a plan is better than a genius without a plan."

Have a plan, even if it is a bad one – getting started is half the battle won.

Self-knowledge is Overrated, Luck is Mistaken for Skill

Daniel Kahneman said,

> "The idea that we don't see, might refute everything we believe, just doesn't occur to us."

Knowledge and skill anyway is not power, it is potential power. Power will come and wealth will be created by how you use the knowledge, the process you follow, the risks you take and the decisions you make along the way. Focus on process and not on outcomes, make the process stronger, automate it as far as possible to rid it of human biases and interventions.

In one of his posts from 2015 in the Wall Street Journal, the American journalist, Jason Zweig, points out that when everyone is skilled at a craft, only luck differentiates how far the successful artist gets. This is true in investing. There are scores of highly skilled investment professionals, fund managers, and even amateur investors. How will then a few of these investors get more returns than others? It is luck. Investing is not like a sport where the most skilled athlete consistently beats others over a few number of games. Investing happens in a randomized environment, which is much different than sports (where a given set of variables matter the most and can be understood and adapted to).

In investing, skill is a must, but it is the luck factor that makes all the big differences. A streak of being right can make anyone forget how important luck is in determining the outcome. Mistaking luck for skill and chance of knowledge is an expensive proposition in investing.

Risk is Manageable, People are Not

Risk is something you don't prepare for and, in most cases, it can actually be mitigated by consulting a good financial advisor, adopting a suitable strategy, and following a process. However, most investors do not do this. Instead, they just follow their instincts, or do what their friends are doing, or lean on what the business news channels and journals are recommending, and thus end up losing their shirt in the bargain.

Always look out for what could go wrong, rather than what could go right. When you are investing your life savings, it's better to err on the side of inaction rather than taking thoughtless action in haste. As Morgan Housel said,

> *"Not every poor investment is the result of a poor decision. No matter your strategy, investing is a game of probabilities. And even really high-probability bets won't always work out in your favor. Just as you can be right for the wrong reasons, you can be wrong for the right reasons ... You can be wrong half the time and still make a fortune ... However, you shouldn't play Russian Roulette even if the odds are in your favour."*

Do Not Ignore Biases

While we all might like to believe that we are rational and logical, the sad fact is that we are constantly under the influence of cognitive biases that affect our decisions, influence our beliefs, and sway the decisions, especially in money matters. Sometimes these biases are fairly obvious, and you might even find that you recognize these predispositions. At other times, they are so subtle that they are almost impossible to notice.

The cognitive biases are common, and collectively influence much of our thoughts and, ultimately, decision-making. Many of these biases are inevitable. There is no way around them except for using systems designed offline with a cool head.

Do Not Lose Sight of What's Important

Ralph Wanger, in his book, *Zebra in Lion Country*, recounts the tale of a man and his dog. He describes the movement and idiosyncrasies of a dog to and fro around its owner. The dog is always excited and is barking and exploring every possible thing, yet it never goes beyond its leash. In the end, he covers the same path as the man which is generally predictable. He analogizes this with a business and its share prices.

While most investors look at the dog, they forget that it is the path of the owner that matters the most. As you navigate your life as an investor, pay more attention to the owner (earnings of the businesses) and less to the dog (stock prices).

At a personal finance level, the dogs are the returns. The owners are your financial goals. For most investors, maximising returns takes precedence over securing financial goals. However, maximizing utility is more important than maximizing returns. Your portfolio needs to be compared with its target value, not with the performance of benchmarks. After all, what good is underperformance or over-performance against benchmark if you run out of your corpus midway in your retirement or you cannot send your daughter to college? Do not lose sight of what is important.

Good Advice Never Changes and is Seldom Followed

Like good advice around health, good advice around money also never changes. It is also rarely followed in both cases.

Every doctor says that to lead a healthy life, exercise regularly, walk a lot, avoid junk food, quit smoking, drink moderately, eat more greens and fewer carbs. Similarly, every financial advisor will say this to be on track in life - make a budget, set financial goals, invest before you spend, start investing early, let compounding work, avoid unnecessary risk, diversify, and be aware of your biases.

As far as our health is concerned, nature has built-in buffers and extras. We are given two of each part of the body and are also given enough leeway to abuse our system and get away with it. However, it is up to us to take care of our money.

Money management needs simple rules. You don't need a magic formula but discipline to win. There are no money geniuses, only emotionally disciplined people who follow a system.

There is No Dearth of Opportunities

Markets will always give you opportunities because investor behaviour is irrational and it creates these opportunities from time to time. Frankly speaking, the crowd just can hold it together all the time. It always swings between a state of panic and euphoria. You just need to be patient for the gaps to open and make a profit.

Steve Jobs said,

"People think focus means saying yes to the thing you've got to focus on. But that's not what it means at all. It means saying no to the hundred other good ideas that there are. You have to pick carefully. I'm actually as proud of the things we haven't done as the things I have done. Innovation is saying no to 1,000 things."

Good investing is all about saying no to countless opportunities and making fewer mistakes. It is not about selecting winners but about eliminating losers. If you patiently say no to most opportunities, and only act when there is widespread panic or euphoria, you will probably spend 20% of the time in-market and make 80% of the returns. This is the most difficult thing to do.

Wealth Can Only Be Created Through a Windfall, an Inheritance, Winning a Lottery, or Through Compounding

Good investing is not about creating wealth but about preserving wealth, about preserving your purchasing power of money. Wealth is best earned from your business, profession, or vocation; you only invest to make it grow. It will pay you to remember that,

> *"Wealth is earned on Main street and not created on Wall Street."*

The stock market is a zero-sum game and gains only lead to claims on that wealth at the cost of someone else. We always tell investors that we don't have any magic wand. We will just try and help you make fewer mistakes and let compounding do the rest. Compounding is when you start making your money earn money for you.

Most investors suffer from exponential-growth bias, which is the tendency to neglect the effects of compound interest, which is what happens when earned interest is reinvested. Research shows that this bias matters. Households with a stronger bias tend to save less and borrow more. They also delay the start of their investments assuming that it will not make much of a difference. Compounding is your long term friend, other than that you need to be extremely lucky.

Know When to Sell

There are thousands of books written on buying assets, but you shall hardly find any on selling. When to sell, the decision is best left to automation, asset allocation, and your advisor. One of the best pieces of advice that we have read on the subject is,

> *"Sell when you need the money and buy when you have the money."*

This holds true on the converse side as well. Investors don't like to accept mistakes. They will hold onto losers and keep selling the winners which Peter Lynch says is akin to,

> *"Watering the weeds and plucking the flowers."*

In investing, as in life, you need to acknowledge a mistake, accept defeat at times, lose gracefully, and exit. As they say in Silicon Valley, "If you have to lose, lose cheap and lose fast so that you can get up and rise to a new dawn."

Black Swans Happen, All The Time

United States Secretary of Defense Donald Rumsfeld once answered a question in a news briefing and gave us the concept of two types of ignorance in this world: "known unknowns" and "unknown unknowns".

We generally don't prepare for the second category, but that is what causes the maximum damage. In the last few years, the biggest headwinds that investors and businesses cared for or estimated for, were oil prices, interest rates, inflation, election results, Fed announcements, and so on, but suddenly the "unknown unknown" Covid-19 happened without announcement and turned the world economy topsy turvy. The basic principles of personal finance were thoroughly tested.

Financial advisors propagate that you must maintain a contingency fund of 6-12 months of expense, have adequate term and health insurance, not use unnecessary leverage, diversify your investment across asset classes, have enough liquidity, digitize your investments, and so on. These tenets all got checked point by point. The actual role and importance of an advisor came through amidst the turmoil and volatility. They helped their investors avoid the impulsive decisions and reap the opportunities offered by the market.

Despite this experience, do you think the world will still be ready next time a Black Swan happens? We doubt it seriously because the form with different dynamics will be different.

In the end, no matter how much money you have, if you are still worried about your finances, you aren't wealthy. Decide for yourself, what being rich or wealthy means to you and act accordingly.

Don't trade away your happiness now to earn money in hopes that if you make enough you'll be able to buy it back later. You can't. Life, after all, is about making an impact, not making an income.

www.ingramcontent.com/pod-product-compliance
Lightning Source LLC
Chambersburg PA
CBHW020735180526
45163CB00001B/252